Create, Create, Create

My second year of poems

Nate Crew

Published January 2023

Dedicated to Amanda.

Life and death both come and go,
but love lasts.

Thank you for being my love and my muse.

CONTENTS

Introduction

By some standards, not every piece in this book can rightly be called poetry. That's the very least I can concede to any future critics or reviewers, whom I expect to elaborate some harsher assessments of their own.

On the whole, I do admit much of this work is lighter (both in quality and mood) than was much of my earlier collection, *The Thing That Heals: My First Year of Poems*. That volume wasn't given an introduction like this one, or a dedication. She didn't seem to need the extra attention at the time, somehow. (I'm not sure if she's jealous or not.)

This book, however, may be a better starting point for anyone first wading into the drivel that I indulgently call poems. So, here's hoping someone eventually relishes some of it as much as I do.

One thing I want to say on this page is to Mom and Dad: I'm sorry if some of the lyrics paint too stark a picture of how far I've deviated from our old straight and narrow. I love you both and laud your good attempts. But I never was much for narrow paths anyway; I'm too clumsy—always used to keep running my bike into trees. Some of us just need more space, you know.

To any other family and friends who may lean further than me toward the moral or conventional side of things, or who may otherwise find fault with some of this book's crude meanderings: I hope our cordial relations aren't damaged too much by your reading this and/or my other poems. But if they are... then stop reading! Anyway, if reading it makes you take me less seriously, that's not an altogether bad result.

I want to thank two friends and local poets, Tiago Azevedo de Mafra and Lauren Tyler. Each of them has helped stir the cauldron of inspiration in the past couple of years.

An old Welsh proverb, *"Gorau prinder, prinder geiriau"*, translates to mean, "The best shortage is a shortage of words." I hope this saying refers to spoken words, not written. Otherwise, I'm a fool and this book is another American atrocity.

Either way, I hope you the reader will enjoy and find a little something worthwhile in these pages, whether in an initial reading or further down the path.

Cheers!

PART 1

"ABSURD" AND LESSER POEMS

LAST NIGHT

Last night I dreamed and it truly flowed
     Ten thousand fluid lyrics
         Not one dry line of prose
With visions dim where I planted sticks
     To see them swell to stalks in
         The perfect spots, the fluid fix

I don't remember a single phrase
     The nights are always fragile
         The sun dries out the days
But if I could write the dream-words down
     The world might call it nonsense
         And label me a clown

MANNA

Open the sweetest fountains

Wandering through dark mountains

Columns of fire and of fog

Walking, just me and my dog

Give me the manna to eat

The midnight so tender and sweet

That opens to me from beyond

And flows from below and then gone

Melted away as a vapor

Caught here a speck on a paper

THIN LINE

Thin line from my pen to you
Or else to myself, it's true

    It rages late

    Around the page

    It won't abate

    Nor fade with age

The ink doesn't flow all night
No thinking in brighter sight
Your light shows a link that's right

    It stretches out

    The line of ours

    It links about

    A ring of stars

A halo around your head
A feeling you've never read

BE A BRIDGE

"A fo ben, bid bont"

"To be a leader, be a bridge"

To be anything worthwhile

Be a bridge

Flexibly solid, spreading, unbreaking

Not forever narrow running

A grinning child headlong swinging

Across a rickety old rope bridge

As a panting little sibling straggles

Running behind, crying to catch up

Stop! Careless child!

Spread your arms

Don't you know?

Ropes break

Dear ones dangle, then fall

Into the chasm of your heart dropping

Into the abyss of wishing

You'd been a bridge

POSSIBLE

But is it even possible
For words to heal so deep a rift
For sentiments and thoughts to bridge
A canyon of such brittle cliffs

The walls oppose each other
The options face their limit
Where mind and body narrows
Closing down within it

In a narrow trench
Cut the marrow bone
Shoo the sparrows
Sit alone

Barely breathe
Sucking air
In too deep
Down there

Fell far

Lay it down

Culvert pipe

In the ground

Stacking rocks upon the top

Climbing on them from the shadow

Bridges take a lot of work

Set them deeper, never shallow

SKIN GAME

You know full well that I am me
And yet my skin is what you see
I know you're you, but I'm the same
The skin's the vision in the game

I know full well that we are kin
And now it's time to let you in
It's cold outside, undignified
A home is warm, a place to hide

I claim no debt for nature's cold
But share a human warmth of old
And feel my skin owes to your skin
A warmer game we both may win

SAFE

"Safe"

"Wholesome"

"Family friendly"

Innocent exclusive words

Exclude a few guilty families or

Whole human expressions that hold

Ideas that feel unsafe to the included ones

Not yet comfortable in their own flesh

Suspicious of a human body's skin

Must safeguard the little eyes

Excluding, burning books

But without real fire

Since fire isn't

"Safe"

LIKE SMOKE FOLLOWS A BODY

Like smoke follows a body around the fire,
My mind follows a body around the senses.
Invisible insinuations filter through.
As yet the breath, the spirit of life,
Has brought to me no higher guide.

Implied in a body's action
Is a movement to outlast it;
Contained in a body's motion
Is an image to survive it;
To me it is given to see it.

Unseen incursion, mystic invasion;
Creators play games of procreation.
A physical frailty may be affixed
To boundless power foreign to physics,
Blindly permeating a bodily motion.

What can avail?
Will starters with finishers be

Eternally at enmity?
Yet again a landscape changes hands.
Here no man kneels to bow the head,
Though an eye blinks in stinging smoke.

Which one will prevail
As thicker smoke pervades them both?
Will a stacking builder ever hear
A grower's whisper in the ear?
One may say I've given way,
Surrendered to a lunacy;
May you follow on a later day, I say.
Yet I begin to hear the fire's tongue,
Here no longer separated like you are,
You standing there, arms crossed;
And better luck to you next time.

Who am I to refuse
To let the body be the muse,
Infusing a union in smoky growth,
Wafting my silent force to follow
Like smoke follows a body.

MAN-SIZE

A fire's heat burns ever deeper
Through the dried-out roots
We watch a flame, the higher leaper
To the sky it shoots

The taproot of the stump is hollowed
Forms a man-size hole
Spark and smoke our vision followed
Ghostly dancer's pole

The low unseen, we see the higher
Balance tilted up
A lightning gave a raging fire
Left a man-size cup

A rain will come and fill the basin
Vase of charcoal black
A mold will grow and green the place in
Ghostly roots look back

RAYS OF SUNLIGHT SLICING DOWN

Rays of sunlight slicing down

Through clouds of harshness dissipating

Beaming open an eye to color

A mind to options after grey rains

Rising like earthworms from below now

To find an expanded horizon

Dappled, green and promising

Where the sky cracked and raged before

April showers bring May flowers, so they say

Some say the Mayflower came only

As a tragedy of history, a human rain too harsh

Converting marshes to cornfields and cities

Slowly now forming deserts

But thunder, understand, had a color, too

Where now I see the brilliant beams

Between grey city clouds

Down to dappled human fields

Rays of sunlight slicing down

TO LOOK UPON THE SUNSHINE IS GOOD

To look upon the sunshine is good
To stay here for another day
See the daylight open into a smile

To hollow out all former expectations
To incidentally find the right route
While holding a loss so hollowing

To wait another day here is good
Together feeling our way back home
Not yet chanting by a graveside

A BETTER VERSE

Today a tree's gnarly trunk
Poured out a sweeter line
Than ever my thinking mind
Drank till its soul was drunk.

Today a frail mushroom head
Spoke out a better verse
Than ever a sage rehearsed
Or any prophet said.

Today a green shaded nook
Showed me a better word
Than ever was read or heard
In any holy book.

WHERE PEOPLE AREN'T

Where people aren't
Stillness is
Punctuating ponderous workings
Too deep to fathom
Too wise to speak

Where people aren't
I pretend
Not to be a person in practice
To be a phantom
A shadow of peace

Where people aren't
Senses wake
Puncture through a tedium shaded
To mind a doorway
To find a key

Where people aren't
Doors unlock

Stairway down to the root cellars

Of new wine flowing

Of angels' mead

Where people aren't

One may breathe

In the misty air of a forest

Relinquish hubris

Abandon greed

WHITECAP ENIGMA

You must increase, but I must decrease

You the louder, lower, destructive

Though goodness flowed only to where

Good ideas were produced on wavetops

Yet for a time, too early and too late

Neglected, your destruction now increasing

Surges to the surface, breaking open

Expanding and contracting slowly

For how long, neither of us knows

A kingdom of hell is at hand

Repentance holds but little weight

Increasing to a new wave after all

My nearer side decreasing only

To bubble out again one day

We froth and bubble together

Between us a whitecap enigma

Ideas burst the surface tonight

Producing more is tomorrow's game

You never saw the surf entire

From the top this way before

DESERT TRIBUTE

Greater love hath no man

Than a willing human shield

Spattered across scorching sand

Mere joking acquaintances in life

Blood brotherly love forever in death

THERE IS NO NEED

There is no need
For it to be you
Doing the deed
And pushing it through

There is no call
For it to be me
Doing it all
Inevitably

Be still a while
Step back and observe
Be meek as a child
Not losing your nerve

Power is yours
In giving it up
Sharing the chores
Passing the cup

Leave the origin be, unseen

The moment you see it, it withers away

Almost seeing through it now

Female landscapes, male implements

Tooling with a change of fate

Almost see, then let it be

BELOVED INMATE

Our years of thick-as-thieves are past.
This is no poem, really.
You're now as un-poetic as
A living person can be.

A rhyme and structure never gave
A life-giving connection.
Your sleeping cell rhymes with a grave
To structure your "correction".

I see my sons soak up the fun
Sandcastles ever youthful,
Like you and me, partners in crime,
To mama, never truthful.

You told me once you liked a girl
The way you liked your coffee,
"Thick and black and strong," you said,
And honest when you told me.

It was a poem etched in time,

Our running, fighting sunshine.

I saw too late; did you go blind?

Or drown it some moonshine?

Our boyhood castle, bridge and moat,

To ruin they were fated.

Your hands around a living throat,

Two orphans you created.

I love you, brother, just as then,

While hating where you headed,

And hope a poem gets you when

You've woken up and read it.

REDEMPTION

You claim redemption in his blood

Without hearing what he really said

Or didn't say

His body went away

A story taking hold

He may have been a God

Yet I doubt he gave you the right

To squash a separate view

Into oblivion

Some view an open heart as cleaner

Than a stern belief

You claim a God's redemption

I ask you for your own

You claim that gods do not exist

That science redeems a future cold

This world is all

Your body will decay

Your knowledge letter fold

A babel tower fall

Buckled underneath all the weight

Of heaven under streets paved

With golden woodchips

Some view an open heart as cleaner

Than a stern belief

You scorn a god's redemption

I ask you for your own

DESERTS AND TREES

Don't know exactly how
Old woodlands used to look
In the places that are now
Barren deserts of Iraq
But it seemed to me
Modern people there
Hope to one day own a tree
Or some cooler, kinder air

Now I'm visualizing
Native forest bounty
In the places now comprising
Lawns and fields of Hoke County
But it seems to pleasure
Many people here
Making for the kids a desert
Mowed and tidy, bare and clear

THAT MOUNTAIN

That mountain was climbed a thousand times

By me

And now

My setting is come, a dropping the sun

To see

Look how

A nightfall is rising, a fading horizon

A smolder, a boulder, a surface, a sliding

I sit

Hard by

The bottom of sloping

Gaze up into hoping

Though lost in the fog of war

My mountain of days before

Is mine when the sun comes up to run

Set free

Redone

To hike and to hold, just like we've been told

To be

As one

A SMILE

A smile

On a dying face

Though climbing out of breath

Breathes more than hills of books

And whether in a room of candles

Or mangled in a smelly mess

The smile never suffers due to

Its lack of words

But words now rise

Translating roughly the smile

For a time when it is mine

"Completion is approaching," it whispers

"Perfection is arising for me

As I lie down

Now seeing how I was born

Exactly as was meant to be

And did and said precisely what was due

And now will breathe a period to the sentence

Seeing deeper how

My book is never ended

But in your veins, child, and your spirit

My life hangs on

And in deeds, books, trees I leave

My soul yet is linking

And in my ripples on the human pond

A heart of mine yet beats

Synchronizing with my spirited girl

Rippling out to embrace the world

And warmer yet than all the rest

A love transports my soul

To where and when is not revealed

Only that soon I

Go freely abroad

Excited now, content because

Although, of course, you cry a while

Completion is approaching

Perfection is arising for me

And soon for you."

So, one day, whispers a smile

On my dying face

BEAUTY TRUE

Alright, alright,

We see you.

Let us cheer and clap our hands

For your winning strength.

How long do we shout and applaud?

Will you be satisfied *then*?

When will the boastful story end?

What more do you require of me?

May I leave?

Alright, alright,

We feel you.

Let us sound a pity note

For your victimhood.

How long of a note shall we play?

Will you be satisfied *then*?

When will the sorry tale end?

What more do you require of me?

May I leave?

Alright, alright,

We hear you.

Let us nod and purse our lips

For your judgement sharp.

How many opinions to hear?

Will you be satisfied *then*?

When will pontificating end?

What more do you require of me?

May I leave?

Ah, there it is:

Beauty true.

I could sit and stare for days

At your hands of grace.

How kindness cleanses the soul.

May you be satisfied, then,

Compassion bless you without end.

What more can people seek to see?

Stay with me.

THE DOGS

The dogs you will always have with you
The barking in-crowds, rough cabals
Every alpha knows it all
Every sagacious knucklehead
Fanatics of a dog-eat-dog nature
Teeth in a tug-of-war backward
As logic is a game they play
Or tennis balls they bounce away
Into ignorance or predation
Each bizarre confusion growls a note
Or howls incessantly upon
Conspiracies of thin air, starlit
As dogged ideology fires the nights
Warm inside from the cold, crowding around
The only comforting glow they know
But you stand friendly by the door
Unenthralled yet graceful, tall
To look upon the panting pack within
Your wagging friends

MEDICINE

Laughter is medicine to the soul

But not always

Sex is medicine, but not always

Silence is medicine, but not always

Food, drink, air, happy children, religion,

Emotion, action, cold nights, warm company

All medicines

But not always

Living healthy soil

Is medicine to the soul

All living healthy soil is medicine, always

FRESH AND DIRTY

Fresh and dirty

Tree-ripened, a dusting of pollen

Blow off an ant, rub off some mud

Squinting eyes, sweating lips

Open up and crunch

Joy dripping down the chin

Sun-worship making love to the tongue

The day is renewed

The body turns its back upon

Packaged clean of store shelves

As summer brings hard falling for

Gifts of a bending tree branch

All fresh and dirty

A RICH NARCISSIST

A rich narcissist in Brazil

Has nine supermodel wives

And God, sometimes I wish I had it like that

But even if I had a trillion dollars

The price of narcissism

Is more than I'd ever want to pay

THE FLESH

The flesh, they say
Is an evil temptation
Homicidal addiction
Pulling to drown you

They live that way
As if only in daytime
Ever serious, no playtime
Sunshine to ground you

Hard shell today
But tomorrow let's crack it...

Light nutshell of rhyme and reason shatters
Under the silent hammer at midnight
Of skinny dipping in the flesh
There you are, I swear you are
You, true, and me, too
They'll call me a serpent for saying it
Say what you will, but

You in the flesh are a goddess

Or a god

Or someone for which we have no word

It's no poison fruit, just magic

The only trick is to chew but then

Spit the pit

Find a neat new nutshell

Cover the flesh at dawn

To skinny dip at midnight and not drown

Dry off and bring your own eternal life

Back into innocent daylight

A MUDDLED MIDNIGHT PRAYER

Of death and wide beginnings

A labor begun

My head in clouded spinnings

Reaching to bleach in the sun

Toward the connection I stretch

The Something, the link

A pressure is swelling to fetch

Where I overthink

Upon my back is clinging

A monkey of flesh

Our bond the song we're singing

Spirit is caught in the mesh

Come drop in my lap yet again

My place in your peace

A fresher plateau where I pen

Links where my thinking has ceased

TRIPPING TO STUMBLE HEADLONG

Tripping to stumble headlong

Into a future of bedlam

Somewhere a shining of heaven

Just over the hill

Is heaven or hell

May look scary, but all is well

May come along with hilarity

Always a singularity

Around the next corner

Skidding and skipping

Never waiting to pick direction

Equilibrium is just an exception

Yes to all, roll with it

Time to let go a bit

Stumbling feet make amends

Tumble in heat, my good friend

Headstrong is weak in the end

PILLS

When will I see

That my enemy

Is not the schemer himself,

But the pill he swallowed?

Pill that told him,

"Conniving is the way to get on top."

Not the zealous cop,

But the pill that drugged him, saying,

"Orderly authority is worth vicious oppression."

Not the politician herself,

But the pill she swallowed that said,

"Control and fame will make you happy."

Not the abusive executive,

But the pill that told him,

"Go on, overreach, take it all, it's OK to be a user."

Not the false accuser,

But the pill that told her,

"Attention and sympathy will bring true comfort."

Not the chest-thumper,

But the pill that whispered,

"Only pride—not humility—is the path to strength."

Not the drama junkie,

But his screen-time pill:

"The sky is falling; be alarmed, be angry."

Not the religious fanatic,

But the hallowed pill:

"To defeat the infidel is God's will."

Hard to see

The real enemy

With so many people

Popping so many pills

But I need to see.

ANTISOCIAL

If tomorrow looks like
One big party,
We'll be parting.
I'll be
With me.

If the future looks like
One big city,
What a pity,
It seems
To me.

It may be as green as
Cities could be;
Still exclude me.
Rather
Be dead.

I mean no offense to
All you neighbors.

I just favor
More room
To breathe.

MYSTERY IN THE SLIME

Maybe once

Outside of time

In the midnight of my spine

Could almost recall a message

In a mystery in the slime

Of being a laughing Celtic god

Hairy belly full of wine

To see you through my trees

A Persian goddess

Or maybe Hindi queen

Sweet mother Mary there you were

And I wanted you because

You were also me

And I did maybe—but I hope not—

Cause offense in drunken glee

Maybe there

Separated from all space

Tangled blue all-out tattoo

There we ran a naked race

You were me and I was you

Under over, over under

But that's all I could recall

For then came Saxon ships of thunder

To me a heavy cross to hoist

Sharp crescent sword to you

And other dark immortals joined

All split and joined in two

Spearmen Spaniards, swift Egyptians

Storming Normans' sterner party

My bowmen joined it, too

Then Māori, Innuit, Mayan, Zulu

My trees go into Moorish ships

Plying seas and prying open

Pandora cans of worms

Water salty, no more wine

Bottle message breaking, broken

Squirm outside the space of time

Memory ships will slip unspoken

Bow to stern they hold a line

In a mystery in the slime

In the midnight of my spine

SPRINGTIME WITHOUT

Springtime without new sex is like

Only half a springtime

Dry cereal at best, no milk

No sweeter flow, no wordless song

No rhyme to bounce the feet

The cereal still has a decent bite

We make do with what we have to

All grown up, doing right, hemmed in

Living a proper prosaic life

On the straight and narrow

But damn

Springtime is meandering and wide

Poking down to the marrow in the bones

"Come out and play, it's time"

What's a good man to do?

PINE SUPREMACIST

"You are not me,"
Says the pine supremacist
To a humble hardwood thicket.
"Watch me grow tall and fast and free,
Dropping my needles and cones;
Needles draw red lines for you,
Cones enthrone only my own."
The gathered thicket nods,
Preserving what it can,
Waiting for its mycelial gods
To reclaim the pine tree's sand.
Decades are dominated by
The pine supremacist,
Not understanding how or why
The future is deciduous.

OLD COLORS

God I love this place

So much it hurts it chokes

Something in the field flower colors

And my neighbors love it too

Black and brown and white and all

Most days there's a quiet purple peace

But you know

There sure are a lot of churches

Flying that big cross flag

Across quiet Dixieland

Steeple bells still ring loudest here

Louder than up North all cold and blue

Church bells here set the same old tone

Stained glass members once did old work

Of separating Dixie neighbors by color

Neighbor separation used to be

Dirty yellow work of crosses burning

Old churches been down here centuries

White steeples look down beige roads at

Green old trees been here centuries too

Grey shade over memories of

Nameless martyrs, noisy mobs

Black Jesus Christs on silent trees

Trumped-up charges and church handwashing

Long after grey uniforms bled their noisy red

Makes me wonder

Old steeples falling quiet now

Will silver silence do more atonement

Than all the loud church bells?

Ringing out so bright and golden

As if Christ wasn't killed a hundred times

On your own brown lawn

Where field flowers silently weep

Their colors run together in my eyes

God it hurts it chokes

God

DREDGING UP

"Why we gotta dredge up
Ancient history?"
A wondering one may ask
"What good does it do me
Hashing out a heavy past?"
Alright, I'll bite
I won't blame you
For I'm a numbskull, too
I write what I have to write
What carries weight
And maybe if you're reading
A past shadow is hovering over you
Unbeknownst but true
Whispering in your ear
Drowned out, pushed down, still near

Present and future fill up the pond
While underneath is what formed us
No man is his own creator
No effect is without causes

Maybe the past needs us to take it

Pull its cadaver out of mud

Up by the bloody collar

Shake it up real good

Hear the change in its pockets jingle

Feel his dead weight

Feel it, own it

Look him in the face

Then plant him in his rightful place

Each generation may have to do it

In their own rough way

Until we're all one race

Or at least until we feel

Each other's weight

BELIEF

Your kind word for folks like me is
"Unbeliever"
Words must be so black and white and
Belief to you must be
Unified, specified
Locked in, nailed down
Never hazy, nebulous, unknown
You're convinced, compact and sure
I'm spread out, scattered
Wild heathen oats
A horndog bum, poor lost soul
Shameless me
Swinging like a spider over fire
On a highway to perdition
Out of step with true salvation
And your way and truth and life
I deny you not and yet
Upon your tighter road
I only hope you know
That lockstep never

Unearthed a key to

Unlock and open

Actual

Shocked

Bedazzled

Bewildered

Belief

AS ABOVE, SO BELOW

"As above, so below"
Say it, pray it, seek to know
Magnets spinning out in space
Raindrops run a magnet race

Quick to feel, slow to kneel
Look above and click the heel
Feet go spinning on the deck
Go below to kiss the neck

As below, so above
Feel the dirt and show the love
Planets swimming through your sea
Critters squirming under me

Small to big, big to small
Bugs to galaxies and all
Never know the role we play
Nor the words we like to say

SPORES IN THE DUST

Spores in the dust in the wind

"All we are" and the song wasn't wrong

Scarcely knowing what we carry

Barely seeing where we've gone

Playing a tune of the breeze

Loosely wound around a windy fate

From the ground comes a sound of release

Dust to settle and germinate

Winding new threads around trees

How did a germ of creating

Sprout from the filth of the feet?

All is vanity and striving after wind

Symbiotic, systematic, sure I see it

Yet let me be just one spore, free

Float up and on, my own gust blown

Chase a dream of hearth and home

Dusty mantlepieces sitting heavy

Land to spread a moldy growth

A web to call my own

ATOMIC GENERATION

I awake into being
To know that I am
My will to act into space
Force coursing through me
I bring in the pretty little sparks
Each one that pleases me into my orbit
Each bosom swelling with a potential world
I shine my will upon their varied bosoms
Each planet and moon of my whirling harem
And I see you, most fertile of all
And in seeing make you mine for now
And in making make you become yourself
Revolve your beauty faster and faster around
I, myself, proton

> An electron is in a process of
> Becoming me, beginning of
> New worlds we know not of
> Your word is spoken upon me
> Set my universe into motion
> Your light brings forth my energy

Breaking into a dance which

You never may control

You powerful pulling force

Acting so heavenly free

Upon electron me

I started your dance to see it run

And there you run away

Into a brighter sun

Out to a newer day

Your universe grows

I become we and we become

The many gathered

The all

OTHER SIDE

My dear reductive kin
Reducing spirit down to religion
Boiling religion down to theology
Stewing to caramelize pungent doctrines
Try eating raw again
Not so smooth and creamy
More vitally eye-opening
      Ever free to return to your stew

And worthy builder friend
Building laws into "law and order"
Raising order to authority's cause
Erecting a cause against all rebels
Try making friends with termites
Follow subversive trails to where
They lead up to decomposition
      Ever free to return to building

And heated destructive child
Destroying strictures that bar your soul

Barring the past from continuing

Passing judgment and breaking stone statues

Try looking at your own foundation

Bedrock past that gave you a soul

Roots of the future's fruits

    Ever free to return to your burning

WATER FLOW

"Toe the line!"

Line up to fill up

Canteens in a desert

Somehow, I, though not in line

Believe I'll still be fine

But how do you know

That I'm not drinking from

The same spring as you?

How do you delineate

From where the water must flow?

Doubtful you know the way I take my drink

Because I don't understand it myself

One thirsty gulp while some

Discard baby and bathwater

Draw lines all you like, but

A geyser sprouts from somewhere

Amazing me every time

Then dry spells in the middle

Sit on my hands

Write not a word

Till the living spring taps in again

I don't know how

You think you know how

Living water flows

But how do you know?

LIFE

Where does our life come from?

> The light, and the breath, and pulse of energy

Where does our energy come from?

> The light, and the air, and all the food we eat

Where does the food come from?

> The light, and the rain, and soil beneath our feet

Where does the soil come from?

> Death and decay

> Away from the light

IT PLAINLY HAPPENED

It plainly happened
But before it did
I was immune to everything
Hard as hickory I was
Standing, touching the sky
Nothing touching me
Through the sinewy bark
Till it happened so plainly

There happens a place
As happens a time
Where thick hickory trees get chopped
What else are axes for?
Whack
Whack, whack
It tickles at first
Then *ouch*
And here is happening
A place to hack it up
In plain and simple words...

It plainly happened
My happy little brother
Clearly wasn't so happy
Standing by his car
When he shot himself
Crack

Boom, a tree crashing down
No punctuated words can ever touch it

And yet beyond my brother
Beyond my hickory stump
It plainly happens all the time
On levels little and large it happens
Chop down memories all you want
But it stands plain and painful clear
That lonely delusions happen
Like desperate defeats happen
Slavery and oppression happened
And mindless, heartless, greedy war
And myriad unfair tragedies

All plainly happen still

Always done by someone

Maybe always will be done

So what's the point?

No point is touching me today

Not in this immune verse

Standing like a hickory sapling

Only happening here to say

It plainly happened

WOODEN NONSENSE

Welcome to the gnostic order of—
Why are you here?

Somehow we have got deal with—
Have you no fear?

Are you not a man and a—
One vacancy now

Secret thought, abandon the—
Let me show you how

Newborn to the triune mission of—
Stand over there

Nonsense of a wooden standing for...
Let there be air

Exhale it somewhere
All, one of us now

What are we born here for?
To do it somehow

Reborn, my hands, and yours
One, all of us now

Plant trees, grow thoughts, end wars

A TREE-PLANTING MEDITATION

Plant trees, grow thoughts, end wars

Bring them all, short and tall, move in force

Retell my mind the thrust

Lay it on, thick and strong, for I must

Never cease, yet remind, till we're dead

Over fields let the groves wider spread

You'll be the numbers, I'll be the force

You hold the rhythm, I pour the verse

Your wordless poem, my silent words

Plant trees by millions

Grow thoughts and end wars

THEY'RE NOT COMFY

They're not comfy

Those hard words in the pages

Sharp and bumpy

Rocky trail of the ages

We walk heavy

Driven by holy voices

We're not ready

Running low on our choices

People hurting

And for nothing, rejected

Kinship burning

Where a bridge was erected

Pay attention

Or they'll steal it in killing

Hard prevention

Can be done if we're willing

KILLER BOY

One
We were
We were all supposed to
To be one
How did he not see it?

One
We were all supposed to be one
How did he not see it?

One
We were born
We were to be one
How did he not see it?
One

"ABSURD"

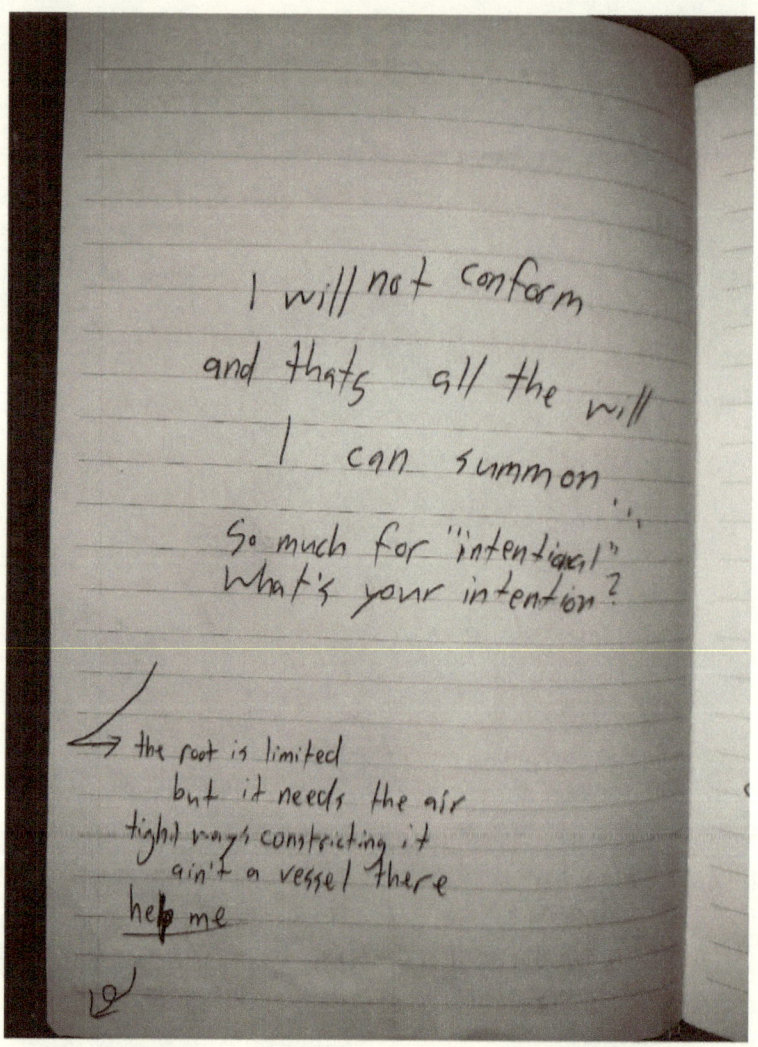

I will not conform
and thats all the will
I can summon,
So much for "intentional"
What's your intention?

the root is limited
but it needs the air
tight ways constricting it
ain't a vessel there
help me

put out the fire with water
they'll hiss at you but it's OK
new dark path of accepted tangles
glowing where you cut them today

it's weaker than yesterday's blaze
    with the reeds
but still no word or image will
    although they may become part of it

Let my hands
    Be your hands

careful, though, watch when it
    turns deep deep red and drips...

but then sometimes I just need to
    be more plain
every man can only feel his own pain

85

haha ha   so let's box it up
to show how it goes
always comes back to
let it come up from below

I can either seep and dazzle in
the steep visual caverns within or
I can intend to cascade onto this page
Why are human relations so steeped
in so much rage

So much work to do
like my invisible spirit father said
So much life to renew
Pushing out so much dread

Nothing of the real relation
is on-demand
It wants to mock and go the
other way alone
So let it go and stand
the viney path will find and
pull it down

To join and meet us here on
common ground

Is that object far or near, so hard to tell
Is the future past the same?
Or was that just hell?

We can burn it up or cool it down
All the power in our minds is found
    Then here we go
    Forget the flames
        Maybe they'll revisit in
        Five hundred years
        Give or take an eternity
    Here we go
    back to the virgin land where she
wants to be
all the life is in the edges
every inch an infinity

Where does the healing end
and the fix begin
When do we ever learn
not to box it in

And that's the trouble with
religion to me
So much blockage
Someone's gotta help me see

Where's the freedom
when there's hell to pay
When's the future
stuck on yesterday
I don't want to refuse her
or deny the sun
To me it feels so blinding
when the day is done

And how long can a trip go on when
I already wandered and stumbled through
a dozen universes this evening
my ego melted away on the floor

And we try to make rules
so thereby make ourselves
redundant
resplendent
in our self-perceived something
i don't know the right spelling
how high can their eyebrows go anyway...

AND let me just step
forward to say let me
be the insane weirdo
today when they
need something
anything
attention
give it to them
or they'll steal it by
killing each other not knowing
it's themselves they're
gunming down
pop pop pop

the end ? ? ? ?

And how long can this go on
Being the bigger goon with a gun
When each time we think
Will this be the one time
We all wake up together
And what will "better" look like?

That's an odd-looking question mark
When Marx marked out of his book
the pull that makes us tick
the pull
the pill
the addiction to kick

But to pull every force to
   the cause
Every habit, addiction, and flaw
To hold out every hope of the soul
Clean and dirty, both partial and
                              whole

And there goes barking again
That dog in the dark
   But then
How do you block him out?
With the human discord
   you feel you could
      do without

For the [insert number here] time
Time to put down my pen
And maybe get some
   sleep tonight
But now there's two of them
   that ain't right
Wait where did the blood come from?
Who shed it first
   how far back in the past
      can possibly be traced
         how to divide up
            the human race

            the dog-eat-dog
            the greedy hog

Each dual connection carries
  its own limits
A thorough collection has
  never been seen
  and there's the
    trouble with
      rhyme
        and
          reason

      enter
      mushroom
      opening to...
Something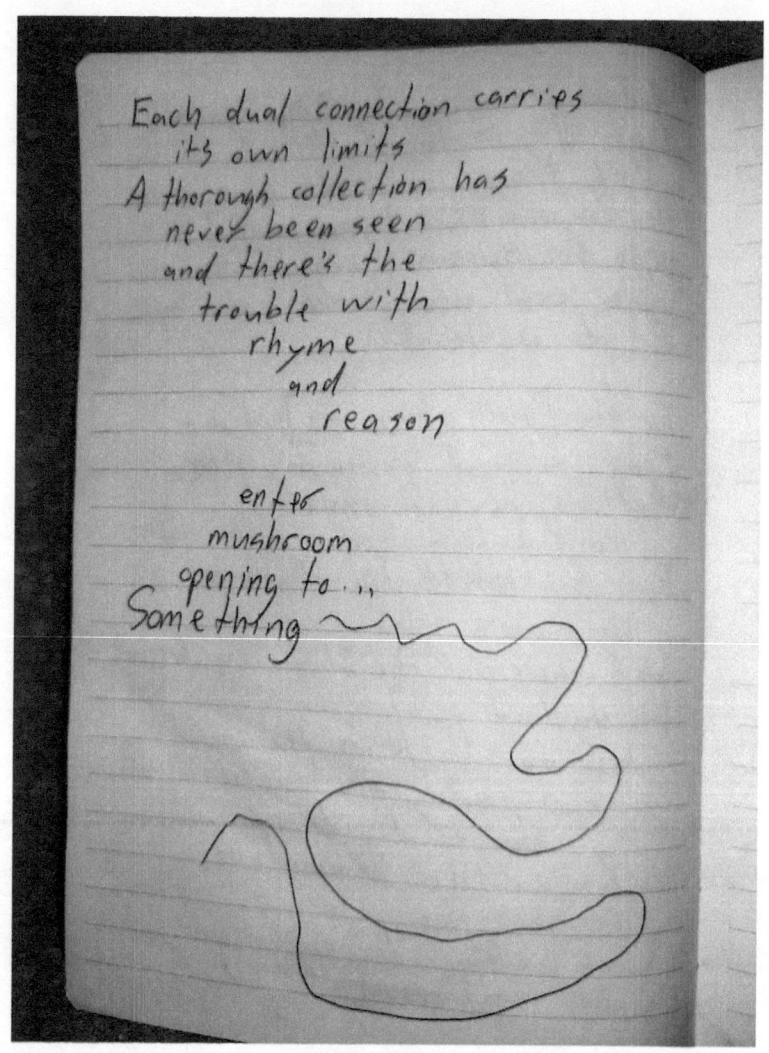

interesting : take note

Ahem: "The energy has unmistakebly
[sic]
    Despite the best of
      (our efforts) wink nod
    Rather than being depleted...
       been recharged !!!

    "How on earth sirs,
    Could we let this happen?
    In our city?
    Heaven forbid
    What a pity

    When we don't
    Any longer
    Own the energy - ""

note taken

"Download" is damn straight
Did this come from my brain?
So then
    What to do
        With the ⌐ profits $$$

Cha-ching
Excuse the dirty word
    my French
    "maid and a foreign chef"
    damn, okay, let me
        watch that

And WHY!

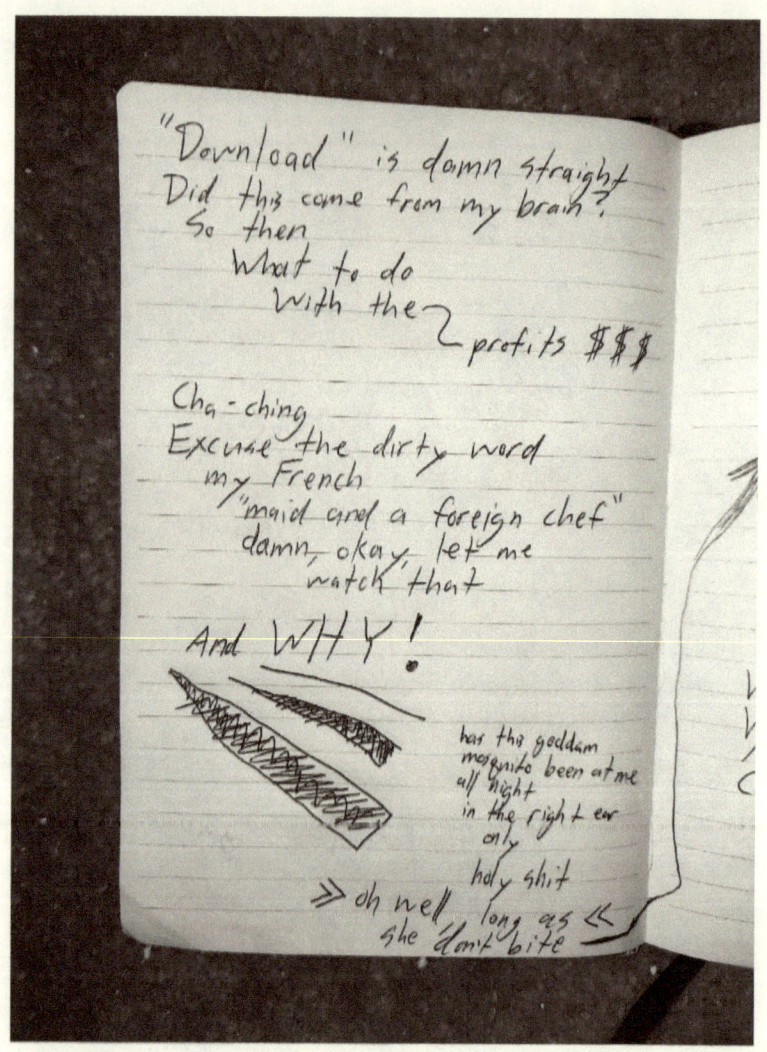

has the goddam
mosquito been at me
all night
in the right ear
    only
    holy shit
≫ oh well, long as ≪
    she don't bite

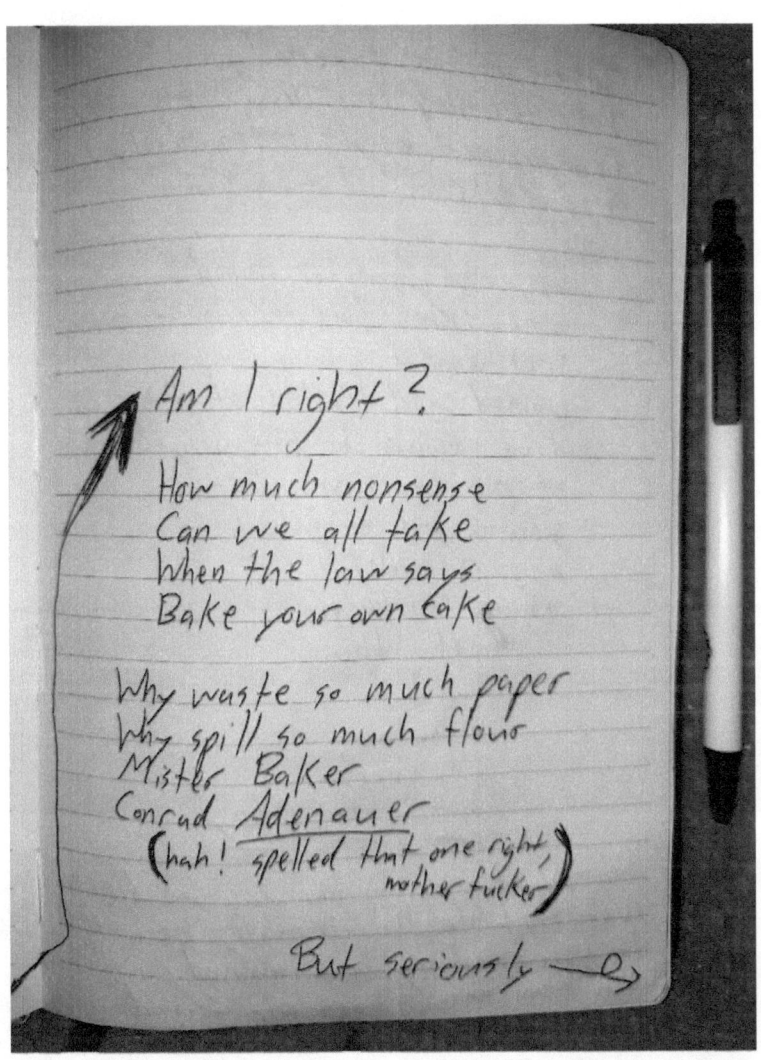

Am I right?

How much nonsense
Can we all take
When the law says
Bake your own cake

Why waste so much paper
Why spill so much flour
Mister Baker
Conrad Adenauer
(hah! spelled that one right,
         mother fucker)

                    But seriously ─◯→

95

Taking nothing personally
Like the slap to Will Smith would be
Crimping each style indefinitely
So... like... I mean...

Oh, okay, never mind
some things forever best being
left unsaid
trained and trailed of the cliff
dive down to the abyss
of not knowing what
you or me or what
anyone would
~~thing~~ THINK
        of this
            but
        however
        forever
        got   to   try

Stopping trying is the day we die
Not that death will really be an end
If you read my book already
You know these lines my friend

96

And abrupt halt into prose
    time to walk outside

=
    "without
        no
            clothes. 。! "

Haha not really, don't be scared
Higher judgement won't be that impaired.
And when I target my wife
    with this gaze
That's between me and her
    that's the way it stays
Just to be clear
    it can never be typed
What is written here
    by no type of big hype

And people wouldn't care
anyway
So a guy got high and
shot all away
Scribbled some nonsense he heard
From wooden voices so—absurd.

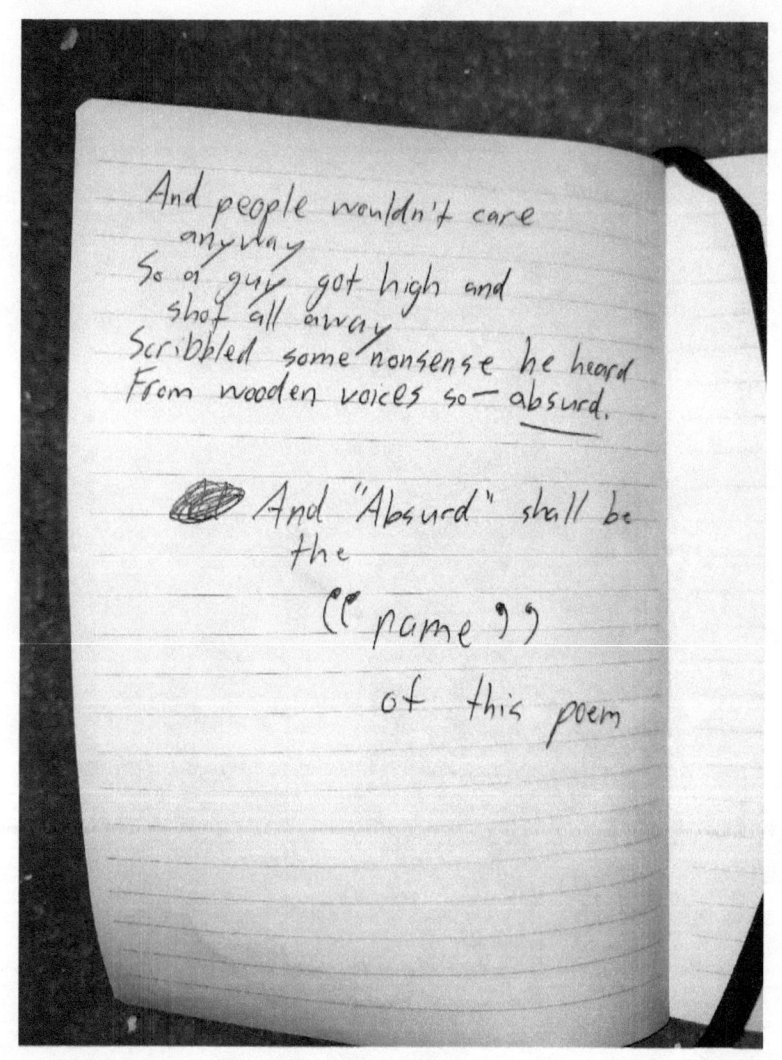 And "Absurd" shall be
the

("name")

of this poem

IS THERE ANY LIMIT?

Is there any limit?

Of course we think there is

Space can hem us in it

And time screws on a lid

But space is only three dimensions

And time, I think, is one

And minds feel safe in comprehension

Of concrete things we've done

Maybe safety satisfies you

It's not enough for me

After diving in the mind through

A sea of flowing free

A mesh of more dimensions

A mind cracked like an egg

Rejecting apprehension

And drinking nature to the dregs

Is there any limit

To nature's force inside?

Once you sink and swim within it

You feel the boundless tide

GO TO THE LIGHT

Go to the light
Might is not right
Hike hills at night
Go to the light

I want to die so bad but can't
Can't leave the family out to dry
Might go insane, might rave and rant
But hanging on, don't ask me why

Why do we fight
Can't get it right
End it tonight
Go to the light

Both yes and no at the same time
I live and die in the same breath
We stop and go on the same line
Both fractured and fractal taste of death

Wait for the day

Hang on and stay

Steer mental ways

Welcome the day

I want to live so bad and will

To give the world a golden pill

Your Golden Privilege is still

The guiding light, the heaven hill

MORNING PATH

Pen to paper this morning

Hard to tell if I'm scoring

A hit or a miss

What will you feel on this?

A hard vision we may see

And how easy shall it be

To loose the ship from its mooring

Beyond the knowledge exploring

Into the unknown

Where the dead men have gone

Or the woman that you loved

Or a little innocent dove

I beat a heavy path with pen and paper

I hope you come with lighter footsteps later

HIDDEN GLEN

Hidden glen
Backwoods glade
Secret clearing
Ringed in shade
Massive trunks
Old as dirt
Whisper wisdom
Love and hurt
Leave it be
Lose it there
Backtrack softly
Taking care
Shady gem
Honey hole
Keep the secret
In the soul

HOLY GRAIL GOOSE CHASE

Surely they told
>   In stories of old
How the Holy Grail
>   Wasn't made of gold
And how jewels never comprised its worth
Plain old cup
>   Of brown old earth

Plainly the goal
>   Of everyone's quest
Was believed at first
>   To appear the best
And among a mass only one will stare
Drink it up
>   A vision there

Blinding, the hunt
>   Of shiny wild goose
And a shotgun pops
>   Eardrums when it shoots

And among a party all giving chase

Only one who

      hears and waits

See what I see

      And hear what I hear

Come wait with me

      Till the rain appears

When it wets the clay, we then may mold

A dirt-poor cup

      For gods to hold

PRESSURE BUILDING

Pressure building
> Back in the skull
>
> Between the eyes

Suction pulling
> Sweeping us down
>
> Whirling to rise

Act of breaking free
> That is the key

More than freedom gained
> Thrill of arrival
>
> Pressure released

Sucked again down in a vortex
> Of bursting forth
>
> Ecstatic birth

Proof is in how you are feeling
> Reeling it in
>
> Casting it free
>
> How real are we
>
> A barrier thin

A death is rehearsed

When roles are reversed

And here is where you feel or think

I lost myself within some verses

You lose me when you swim, so sink

And linger not upon the surface

      Of transcendent waves of nonsense

      On occasion dipping back in

      Coherent shallow waters

      Intelligible phrases

Then sink again to waken

To read a pressure building

Acting out, casting free

Releasing as you read

The other person

THE PAPER

"Know the paper will understand"
Spoken urge of a broken man
Any old paper may know
Even a screen and keyboard may go
But not in reliable ways
Never predictable, subject to change
Here and there a puzzle piece
Makes its way to here release
Onto the paper

You know paper fades away
Tomorrow the words are gone
Maybe lost already today
So if expressive urging on
Fails to take a message through
What does it mean anyway?
                    "Why don't you just come out
                    And say what you really mean
                    Or stop slinging words so carelessly?"
What I mean?

What do *you* mean by standing there

All narrow, all action, all under control

Look here and see pieces of yourself

Falling and rising, cracking and mending

A humanity may come apart at the seams

Like pages come loose at the spine

And if it's me disintegrating here

It'll be with a pen in hand, not a gun

With any hope and love I may gather

In place of crackling fear or fury

The mind cracked open once before

And through the opening still flows

Don't ask me what it means

Streaming hopes out of control

Onto the paper

ARWAIN (LEAD ME)

Lead me through the dark old draw
Wilderness of no spoken light
Frogs and crickets are deafening
Unseen thorns slicing skin tonight
Vines twist and snag the mind
And murky waters chuckle, sour
Squishing in the soaking boots
Hour on desperate, prickly hour
Lord, guide my wandering trek
Through a valley of a shadow dim
When all falls down around me
And I know not where I'm going in
Where dark has pierced my soul
Now you pierce through the murky mist
To speak lightly and lead me
Through a nameless wilderness

GREAT EXPECTATIONS

Great expectations

Sly preparations

Stretch like a net

Bank to bank of a river

Memories and hopes

Lining the slopes

Checking for holes

Reaching to catch

A fish for a frying pan

Great perspiration

One man can only stretch so far

With the hands or heart

Only open so wide for a while

Then sew shut the holes

Spread the ragged net

Wear the worn-out mask

Of great expectations

LITTLE BY LITTLE

What is violence?

    "Death"

Where does it come from?

Little by little

    "Little man, you don't like me?

    Fine, I don't like you either

    Have a knuckle sandwich"

Don't I know?

Death is bound in life and love

"Do what you love," they say

"And you won't work a day in your life"

    And they dismiss

    The homeless addict

    Who does exactly this

But in between his destitute freedom

And opposite poles of productive tedium

Here we waver in desperation

Off on a midnight bike ride

Echoing down city streets

Where the junkie shouts

"What is violence?"

"Death!"

"Where does it come from?"

"Little by little!"

HOT BLOOD

Can't you hear my silent shout
Begging you for freedom
Hoping that you'll kick me out
Hating all your boredom

Don't you know I love to hate
Hate to love and keep you
Turn me down to hold and wait
Keeping me in limbo

Take your own or give me mine
North Pole to South I offer
Life is cold, we're short on time
My blood is running hotter

Loathing fences where I live
Like chafing dogs on leashes
Freedom is but relative
And hot blood finds releases

MAKING

Somewhere in our flowing arteries

Lie the genes of the makers

Of Stonehenge

Links across millennia

And in the veins of our progeny millennia after now

Will be something of us

And what will they be making?

And here in our middle

What are we making?

EXPRESSION

There you are
I see you
Through the noise
Past foreign expression
Underneath it
Even if never meeting
Here beginning to feel you

Here I am
My large print
Reckless swings
Broad strokes
Cryptic thoughts
Crude expressing
Where expression is born new

A midnight moment where we
Imprint ourselves in eternity
We see what they may never see
Sweat is expressed, drenching me

Damp is the heat, dimming sight

Grinning I wade into thickets at night

Hacking and chopping down

Each snake arising now

Attack of dark doubts become good

In foreign briars and woods

Of broad expression

HARMONY BORROWS

Why can't I
Write it better, not so vulgar
Fine love letter, "have and hold her"
They may say
Smooth it over, sweep it under
Drop the older, squelch your thunder
They don't know
It will never stop
Thunder cracks their smoother glass
Jungle sprouts through newer cracks
Harmony borrows, renting the time
Animal comes, collecting each dime
Civilization, a house of cards
Cycles of shatters, of flying shards
The gravitation pull never ends
It tends to bend my pen to the trend
Not of finer love's elation
But of chaos and creation

GRASSY PATH

If the road to hell is paved

With the highest of intentions,

Will the grassy path to peace be laid

By the plodding institutions?

Where they plod and chew the cud,

Herding slowly into greener pasture,

There they play a part, but in the mud,

Heaven's grassroots, peace is growing faster.

On the other hand, I might be wrong.

Peace may fail to be a growing song,

But arrive in clouds, a blinding blast;

Institutions then become the past,

When all bets are off and states are gone

And no way to mow the White House lawn.

Here they come again, the grassy ways;

Silent nights begin, and humbler days.

ONLINE DRAMA

Screens of meme conspiracy

Screams and mindless tyranny

Soak in facts to wring your hands

Steep in details, blame the man

Us and them, find a team

Form a tribe, make a meme

Lose yourself to stir the pot

To find your soul

       Just shut it off

PUSHING THE ENVELOPE

We never reach the end of the rope

Forever pushing the envelope

And why should we stop it today?

As long as we push the right way

We push it back around to see

It's back where it's supposed to be

LOUDEST

The loudest talking heads
All own the biggest trucks
Ripping up the road
To nowhere as they carry us

I write before I talk
And write before I eat
Hopping off the truck
A fool enough to feel the heat

I'm writing in my sleep
Try not to be too loud
Straining in the heat
Then raining from a silent cloud

A bullhorn takes a stage
The thunder wakes the birds
While in fertile brains
The dead awake in silent words

That driving hard and loud

That blowing hard hot air

Dazzles empty crowds

The slogan shirts with nothing there

We question all the talk

A reckless open door

Jumping out to walk

Though hot outside, we're finding more

LET ME

Let me dangle

       I mean it, really, please let me

       My tension line between two poles

       Between a lonely liberty

       And warm connection of our souls

I like to walk the line

At times I miss a step

So let me dangle, I'll be fine

I'll get my balance back

Let me bend to

       The limits of the love in me

       For if it's high, with sacrifice

       I balance love out sensibly

       Preferring goodwill's lower price

Acknowledgement or thanks

Pick up where love leaves off

Take up the slack, I climb the bank

Not slinging love like rocks

Let me stand up here

    To dignify, appreciate

    You from a distance, not so near

    The magnet strength, the love or hate

    Too much for me to bear, I fear

I like my open space

My high tightwire walk

You do your thing, you run your race

I'll meet you at the top

Let me be me

    Although they turn the tables sharp

    Remembering to signify

    The skin as my defining mark

    The splinter's out, look in the eye

I'm more than just a race

High balance in the sun

Let me be me, we're face to face

Let you and I be one

WHAT FIREBALLS

What fireballs are these

Pressing up toward the surface

Of safer paper consciousness

What poison darts or burning arrows

To pierce a tepid shell of routine

If you draw them out too soon

You'll miss the heavier mettle

As it slips back out of reach

Be a big boy

Don't act scared

How many words of these

Embers in the wind

To burn into half a poem?

Where does one begin?

The edge wears off over time

A charcoal smudge rubs off

A grudge dies out

All those years of thinking too hard

Doing too much

Working too submissively

Pursuing a happiness which

Is bound to escape you and me

At least one key may not escape

A knowledge, let it filter in

That life and liberty aren't safe

And safety's less than paper-thin

HEALING WORDS

Give me the healing words
Cycles of worms and birds
Rhythms of grasses and trees
Bring me the words in the breeze

Let me then give them away
Thoughtlessly in the same day
Words to us come and go
Sending a healing flow

Use them to cover the blood
Screams fade away in the flood
Torrents of words in old tears
Mending the rips of the years

Scatter the healing lines
Wherever the climbing vines
Reach into ponderous trees
Scatter my words to the breeze

TO A LOWLIFE ON RUSSELL ST.

You menaced a lone stranger

    In the dark

For fun and proud earning a

    Friend's regard

"Better watch whatcha doin'," you sneered

      But when a round chambered

      Your friend got weird

      Your threats grew pale in the light

And a warning round flashed

    A flutter of fright

Then the stranger faded off

And your folly returned

As you misunderstood

His shot was not

A thumping chest

But a quick rebuke

    To the route you choose

        Not watching yourself living life

        Not rightly using the night

THE TROUBLE

The trouble is in the limitation;
Peace was always a jumbled-up dream,
Gibberish on a crumpled-up mind,
Where an occasional moonlight ray
Stains divinity onto the course of history.
I used to have organized thinking
With no dimmer evening inspiration;
Old solitude was too bright and shallow,
Unaccompanied as yet by the profound.

The trouble is our own selves;
We keep on pushing the same old buttons
Till the trigger finger is callused,
Thinking we and our skills and equipment
Could dominate the earth.
But all of that borrowed equipment
Only opened a path, paved an entrance
Into bigger and better places
Where the same old ways
Turned into dead ends.

The trouble with beating swords into plowshares

Is that you always want new land to plow up;

The trouble when you don't train your children in war

Is when someone else's child finds an easy target;

And the trouble with us peace mongers

Is that we seem blind to the limitations,

As if in childish naïveté toward human nature.

The trouble with the dream which satiates the soul

Is that it clashes with daytime's insatiable wants;

The trouble with nighttime visions so endless

Is that waking reality brings beginnings and endings.

But the trouble with dismissing the dreaming vision

Is that reality runs deeper than daylight excuses,

And a future may shatter our limitations.

CLUMSY

Words make such a clumsy instrument.

If only I could make colors dance

Infinitely on an inspired canvas,

Or fashion music, or flow my body

To show what letters never can;

If only I could give my living gaze

To anyone regardless of letters.

Oh well; I suppose

Giving my neighbor a peach will do for now.

WHERE DO THEY GO?

The giants of Gath

And heroes of Greece

The men and the myths

And legends of beasts

Half-man and half-horse

And gods of the isles

And those of the Norse

And south of the Nile

The stories we've spun

And visions we tell

The moon and the sun

And heaven and hell

The fables we read

Half-feel and half-know

Just where do they lead

And where do they go?

LIGHTENING UP

Always good to lighten up, but
Seldom does lighter air
>   Breathe true poetry
A burden to bear
>   That makes you free
Breathing in and out
>   The energy of you and me
Always fine to joke around
But finer minds are seldom found
>   Stuck on comedy central
Lighter laughs can blow off steam
But poems draw out life
>   And stitch together dreams
To wear when breathing heavier air

PRIDE AND PAIN

Pride and pain are buried deep

In Southern ground

In with them among the roots

Is comfort found

Not the same in what we do

Biology won't bow

Underneath it I and you

Are part of One somehow

INVISIBLE EAR

Sing, muses, in the invisible ear.
Bring out the moments you want me to hear.
Snatches of movement go timelessly by.
Catch them for someone's invisible eye.

Moments to kneel and then decades to stand;
Filter them through the invisible hands;
Flashes to banish a fear of high wrath;
Radiant conscience to find a bright path.

Sing to me, sing to me, spin me a tale.
Your revelation will never go stale.
Either embodied or floating in air,
Bring me your breath and I may even share.

WHEN THE SILENCE

When the silence is empty,
Its emptiness becomes a whirlpool,
Sucking the life from an entire day.
But when the silence is full,
Its fullness flows into a fountain,
Slaking thirst, washing pain away.

When solitude is lonely,
Its loneliness casts a shadow,
Blotting out the moon all night.
But a solitude connected
Glows from everywhere's source,
Each blade of grass shining at you.

Ah, for the love of everything,
Stay with me, fullness I found;
Linger, connection I knew.
Oh, for the sake of love,
Let me not turn away from life,
Nor yet again dislike everyone.

ALL-CONSUMING BANALITY

All-consuming banality

Wheel-spinning futility

Newer house and a shiny car

Never bother to think too far

Money, money, and more, and more

Busy, slaving, whatever for

Seasons turning and time rolls on

Junk is here and then junk is gone

Go consume at the superstore

Go and get yourself even more

Never sit on the ground and stop

Always pushing to reach the top

Pass the Joneses and win the race

Rats in labs in a frantic chase

Hard pursuing a softer chair

Hardly sitting to breathe free air

FENCES

Fences are sometimes
Existing for some vines to climb
That side's yours and this is mine
Worthless waste of human time
Fools' dividing lines

So let us laugh before we leave
Tear down a fence, erase a line
Wear the heart upon the sleeve
Call many things both yours and mine

PART 2

I WON'T TAKE THEM BACK
AND WEIRDER POEMS

CALLING CARD

Prolific sloppy optimism

A pumping flashing gnarly rhythm

My calling card to you

Be kind to see it through

A broken mirror, see your image

A crooked line, I see a grimace

One seed in here is yours

One key to mental doors

RECONCILE

Far too many years
Turning blind away
Sheltering the ears
From nonsense

Far too much to sense
Blind and deaf and mute
Tight and sure and tense
And flailing

Far too sure to fail
Far too strong to give
Way too right to hail
The wrong ones

Breaking down the years
Making up the time
Sweeping out the fears
Of nonsense

A MAN'S CYCLE

When he rose for seizing the day
Then he gave himself right of way
With the sun becoming his friend
And the moon became a dead end

When he grabbed the bull by the horns
Took a task for which he'd been born
Then the bull said, "Leave me alone"
And the man to ruin was thrown

When he sat alone in the woods
As the moon was flashing her goods
There he found more natural ways
Till he rose for seizing more days

THERE IS NO PUSH-BUTTON

There is no push-button

You can't turn it on at will

Humility is the lesson

And sometimes

You can't turn it off, either

Did I ever aspire to be this way?

Clumsy heart-on-a-sleeve poet?

I was supposed to be a big mean tough guy

But the lesson knocked me down

Turned on, in its own frequency

And if you're lucky enough

It'll turn on to you, too

BE GOOD

Sit still to hear the prayers.

      Be good in stale air.

Grow up to sell your wares,

          And always do the chores.

Don't talk to strangers, please.

      Let God provide each need;

Crawl to Him on your knees

          And bow your guilty head.

Keep schedules, fold the sheets;

      Say grace before you eat;

Don't be the one who cheats;

          And never look at whores.

No burps or slurps or farts;

      Just play your pious part

And dodge the devil's darts;

          We'll pat your little head.

"Dad, Miss Solomon told us we should never say something's ironic unless we can explain logically why it is. I asked if she could explain intuitively why that's a good rule. She looked confused and said to stop asking sarcastic questions. I wonder if she knows how babies are made."

Oh, keep the spirit pure.

      Your needs are met, be sure;

Yet wants you must endure,

          Like fruits a bit too fresh.

Forget forbidden fruits,

      Give Uncle Sam his loot,

Say thanks to all the troops,

          And swipe your credit card.

Stand up, recite the pledge;

      Now kneel, the preacher said;

Stop playing on the edge

          Of dangerous mind and flesh.

Don't venture far at night,

      But fight the noble fight.

Please wear the seat belt right;

Don't drive too fast or hard.

"Mom, my boss said if I consistently install more doodads and take less down time, I'll eventually get a promotion. He felt good about advancing himself that way. I wonder how long till he more or less commits suicide."

Oh, make a pretty house,

Oh, keep the weather out,

Oh, be a faithful spouse,

And bore yourself to death.

Do not offend your kin.

Don't let the devil in,

Nor look upon the sin

Of naked hips or thighs.

Deny yourself to tears;

Stay safe to hide your fear;

At least for 80 years,

Please hold a shallow breath.

What noble, lovely lands

    We'll have if every man,

While sitting on his hands,

    Is good until he dies.

DROPS

Squinting the eyes
Face to the skies
Hand as a visor
He frowned in surprise

Careful what she wished for
Sky grew black too fast
Drops from out of nowhere
Clouds will crack and flash

The trick is to let it flow
To open and just let go
Sometimes it pours
Sometimes it holds
Most times it drips
Small drops of soul
Allow if it wants to dump
No need to become a pump
It knows the channel
Cuts the way

A streambed ancient

Washed out today

It cleanses the mind of dust

It shows you the self to trust

Rainwater flows to the hollow

Low-lying spots overflow

Gain never comes with a warning

Storm gives you more than you know

I WON'T TAKE THEM BACK

Fickle nerves and funny bones

Tickle nouns and verbs

     Walk on eggshells, dodge the stones

     Thrown in wars of words

Male and female seem to be

Minefields of today

     Redefining what you mean

     Holds the truth at bay

Times will change and words will move

Folks may learn to laugh

     Rhymes will step on someone's toes

     I won't take them back

YOU CLIMBED

You climbed the mountain you saw best.

You chose a path and passed a test;

The long ordeal, the brutal climb.

You gave the sweat and took the time.

They may not favor the deeds you chose,

The acts you savored, the way you rose,

The days you seized and the nights you kept.

Your noise offended them while they slept.

STOP BEFORE

Stop before we mine the ore of every vein of life that drains. Peripherally at night, I saw something almost human, holding elemental earth in one hand like a shield of peace, wielding a pathfinding boldness in the other hand like a sacred axe. Backward and forward both, stopping to sense surroundings, then going out impossibly again.

Spin aside and let them ride the bandwagons and passing trains. I saw many of us out of step, going together backward and forward at the same time.

Back toward a faith both more and less, not alternatingly, but simultaneously. Tonight, I'm supposed to write something else, but I don't know what. More talismanic, more attuned, more elemental; less dogmatic, less insistent, less built up. Back to where a cross met a totem, but then forward, forward, forward hard.

Stepping forward, step out far, out of line to raise the bar. In life I'm supposed to do something else, but I don't know how. I somehow do it every day, like you do, impossibly. If it's not a poem, I don't care because here I am at night, back into our peripheral Something with you.

Something outside it all, but in it. Something that appears nothing but is altering everything. Something like an unknown seed of all. Some claim to know, personalizing the Source that radiates and emanates untouchable, unknowable manifestations. All I know tonight... one of those myriad manifestations is the universe we reach to measure with rulers like physics and chronologies like stop, go, stop, limitations. But nothing ever stops.

This universe goes on haltingly emanating its own myriad twists and turns, one of them being our own green world, biology's sphere, where elements dance to the tune of a bubbling energy cycling around, from masculine to feminine and back. Fire, air, water, earth. Sun's fire, wind's watery breath of life on the earth. Pregnant breath you're breathing onto this paper.

In the green reality is where we most intimately touch the Something. In here, in our tiny mental reality, even personalizing earth, water, air, fire may hold up better, a humanized story spun the world over, as the various couplings between four cycling forces beget each new force in principle just as truly as the sun rises each morning with the spin of our green speck. Balance, tension, rhythm, clash, clasping, harmony against melody with a smattering of dissonance. Human hands and bodies, deeds and fertility like yes, no, yes, possibility. The fertile feuds all raging immortally beyond us.

Peripheral nonsense late at night, where something is somehow in there for me to write. But that's all I can squeeze out today. Better stop before spinning away.

THE ESSENCE

The essence of

A giant oak,

Without a word

One day it spoke

To one who heard

The wordless tale

Which books won't hold;

It's far too frail

To be retold.

The books of later

Gods were made

Of oak tree paper,

Slaughtered shade,

And bound in hides

Of quiet beasts

Who gave their lives

For men to read.

But on this page

I cut you free

To prior ages

Of older trees.

Look through the leaves

To see the core

Of wordless essence,

Of something more.

UR

Near where the ziggurat of Ur

No longer overlooks green gardens

Before jihadis bid to erase Chaldean speech

Somewhere a meager yet aspiring intellect

Was sprayed on the side of a Humvee

None of the young red mist tainted his PlayStation

Home where a little brother inherited Call of Duty

Acting like time wasn't precious

And gold-star girlfriend got a new golf investing man

Didn't know about Humvees but look at his Hummer

It could be all made up but you know it's true

And has been since before it happened or didn't

Maybe it's all babel when Assyrians chant a mass

Maybe nothing lasts until the past

Swings around a sundial shadow

Where a forward observer called the shots

Sweat on binoculars making flies curious

Thanks for visiting, say the stones

Our tower was something once

But the translators are all dead now

Nimrod took their heads with style

That princely motherfucker made a name

And maybe the best thing to be at peace

Is not understanding a word of it

As word games always played on the edges

Of insanity vs. cowardly tug-of-wars

It's easier to laugh silently in the hide site

Blurry hindsight lying on his belly for days

All breath reduced to a crosshairs

Writing notes where life trickled down the tower

No I wasn't up there myself back then

Except that we all were up there once

Damn it was hot for Abraham

EGOTISTIC

Me, me, me, me
How egotistic can a writer be
Guilty as charged, shaking my head
Let it work through the system
Forget what you've read

LETTING GO

there i was clinging like a neanderthal onto a branch of a drumbeat like i had hands for feet pitter-pattering on the stretched-out skins and bamboo. holding on swinging in sync in heat just to share a meeting beat with more of you all where it had to mean something in other words match a shape we recognize from his cave-drawn stories of shapely things. shake your head at my fingers releasing the charcoal beat to freefall into never landing nor sounding familiar tunes on the way down around the nature of other-side reality. stay hooked and don't hate a hooking habit when this is how it links to the far branches you hadn't noticed yet, don't cut them, that's me over there now.

FRAGILE NIGHTS

Tripping words

Fragile deep nights

Leave you reaching

Fading dream sights

Boil it down

Dew of morning

Mourning drowns

Shallow or deep

Awake or asleep

Nights releasing light

Eyes to open

Simply knowing

You're alright

YES NO YES

Befalling at least one Parent
      Forced by love to be a No
Despite every Yes inherent
      Repeating stop while meaning go
Or ceding a weaker welcome
      Warm and kind and soft of mind
Surrender a fuzzy outcome
      Find in love more heat than shine

      Long-gone, a seeder who said,
        "Though sweet to the eye,
        A bore in the bed."
      In-laws in a lawless home...
        The rug was pulled out;
        Someone should've known.

Swimming in learning like Auden
Meaning the same as the meaner
Racking up vices like Hefner
But thinking that logic is cleaner

Adam beginning was Be and Go

God being Yes and saying No

"God is love,"

Thought a frightened fleeing daughter.

"God is logic,"

Felt an apologist with high blood pressure.

"My mistake,"

Mused a vice victor after slaughter,

"Was to make

A wife, to love the weak, the lesser."

No-love and Yes-love and runaway victors

Right answers, errors or drunken old quitters

Almighty wee nymph mothers

Puny Zeus players drained of zest

American family gameplay

Phony shades of cobbled love-quest

And heady Auden had one of his girls say,

"Lies and lethargies police

the world / In its periods of peace.

What pain taught

Is soon forgotten."

And if Hindu astrologers get a nod

For some frankincense to the tiny God

    (Though giving not a penny

    To Saint Paul's shouting frenzy)

Might I get a pass for a grenade I bring

At least if it's not a lie-like thing?

    Like higher poets, I

    Let loafing cheap shots fly,

    Let pass as bomb arguments

    Some vague and haunting sense.

Not sorry as long as she liked

What poetry did at night.

There's truth in a lazy haze

As much as in sweaty days.

Parental mental tongue-tie knots

Begotten one poem-conceived night

Where embryonic images were the sperm

Swimming from where love rarely says No

Where God is love and Yes shall win the day

BOUNDING

Like the bounding of white-tail deer

Lightly rounding the bend, disappear

Leave as freely as devil-may-care

Going easy as doves in the air

Desert nightmares are better forgot

Greener pastures of morning thought

Hunters and the hunted both

    Afflicted by crimson dreams

Shedding them, arriving with sunrise

      Bounding lightly away, it seems

MORNING DEW ON THE SKYLIGHT

The night was tenuous and fleeting

And didn't make real sense

"But the world is run by those…"

Who never absorbed poetry anyway

Nor soaked in Bob Dylan's melody

Nor felt the drops filter into

Aretha Franklin's earth

Nor learned to be human at night

VROOM

VROOM goes the engine in all the directions

Lately it's a matter of inclusivity

Including good alongside mediocrity

Specially to those who'll thank you for it

Fuel an escapeful weekend...

Oh, cut the shit, what's the use

You know I do what we all do

"What's a hype" is what I say, is it?

Hah! Got a piece of you now

You squirmy genius Tarantula charmer

God knows experience takes the acid cake

Take all the thrills you can for God's sake

Get tired and take a pitstop break

Then don't crap on our breaktime questions

And don't pretend there's no engine pulling it all

GUTS AND QUITTING

Intestinal fortitude

Systemic exactitude

Clearly defined terms of stubborn idiocy

Till a nipple slips in a smile to see

On a navel ring shining a retort

Blinding high-wall resort

Orphans shine your pompous shoes

Spewing thoughts of you don't care

Better to put each garbage line in print

Than miss a note we should have hit

Laces drag as Johnny flicks a booger

How convenient for us all it would be

If he grows up into dull ruin

Black-tie determination

To wipe his own butt and not be miserable

Little white lies at the cashier station

Colorful candy store temptation

Curate collections of silent impressions

Dismissed by fortified jesters

Shoe-black abstract in extracting from nooks

Crooks in the creases of brain

Criminal pieces down whitewater drains

"Roll black water won't you keep on"

Intestinal Mississippi in the syllables

Myrtle fundamentalism

Murder underneath the system

Walls around what the hell they mean

Johnny don't cooperate

Stream of subconscious — no-not-a-stream

Stuttering broke-up bits of a dream

Fortitude smashed on an impression

Poets are liars, evil beasts, lazy gluttons

Quitters to be exact

Inexactly just looking around

For nipples to slip out of consciousness

And dull ruin to shut its mouth

GOTCHA

Come along now
> Don't drag

Just ignore the
> Red flags

No one reads the
> Fine print

Be a sport, take
> A hint

Accept the money
> Sign here

Congratulations
> You're clear

Dignity?
> What's that?

Who cares when your
> Wallet's fat

We'll respect you
> Don't you worry

Now jump through our hoops
> Come on, hurry

CRUMBLING

In skin-tight visuals

Of rarely literal

A people's greed is crumbling

New frontiers of populist tripping

Flipping a tale back on yourself

Let high priests chase their tails in circles

Vapor trails of thoughts in flight

Barely literal until one night

White marble pillars collapse

Under the weight of underdogs' rage

Beware the mayhem when greed gives way

LET THEM

Let the woman be a woman
She may be narrow, wide or lean
Tight of lips or mind wide open
See her, a goddess and a queen

Let the man be fully man
Let him push for something more
Let him rise to bigger things than
Cars and sports and mine and yours

Then let those who float between the two
Play their note and live their dream
Let them live as you know how to do
Let us see and then be seen

CHARGING

Taking it all too seriously

Guilty as charged

Charging along with no subtlety

Gesturing too large

Give me a moment to read your note

In the lines around your eyes

In a corner where you silently hope

For words to give you rise

Words may fail to fuel the pride

Of writers charging hard

Laying down a track for others

Who inherit taking charge

SOMEONE'S DESPERATION

Audience of one or fewer

Every time

Give me your eyes, your view

Light of your mind

    And there it was

    Loss of all you counted on

    Hung up your harp

    Wept a stream in Babylon

Sands trickle

Glass tunnel

    the bottom dropped out

    rug disappeared from under

    a rugburn way of living

    where do i turn now

    when knees are worn out

    the kids lost faith already

    god help us remember

    surely the darkness won't

    hold us forever

    no, connect the dots backward

grains of sand in reverse

     Click back into a purpose

     Play the past on the harp

     Faith wasn't meant to hurt us

     Though menacing stars

       align in the dark

         remember light hearts

THE POINT

People can be counted on

To disappoint

Until the point is the person

And even then

The eager wonder of a child

How reliable is it?

It flips to mindless chaos on a dime

The beauty of each flip side

Reliant on being unpredictable

Poking through your smooth fabric

Like an arrowhead intrudes

Where the point is the person

REMEMBER

Thoughtless repetition

Feeling notes you know by rote

Chanting in an elder tongue

Tasting ancient flavors

You might read what someone wrote

Or simply find the part of you

That still remembers

HEAVY DUTY

heavy duty

isn't all duty heavy out here?

like a duty to punctuate

be punctual

or to capitalize

letters or else

time, effort, ideas

into financial capital

for what

save or invest or make

maybe a legacy

how happy my long-gone dust will be

to be recognized

when all i really did

was punctuate and capitalize and

collaborate with other grownups

to

ruin the wonderful world

nope

duty and legacy are overrated

the easier yoke

the lighter burden

are in there somewhere

got to find them

PAGES TURNED

To some passersby, each new page turned

Looks like a book closed

Each new evolution

Looks like decline or retreat

Each adjustment in course

Like quitting

And each shift of tactic

Like a loss of focus

Too bad the passersby are only passing by

And don't read books

Now where's the free-flow, where'd it go?

Find it, leave no page unturned

WHEEE

Caterpillar rolling down a slope, *wheee*

Holy roller butterfly diamond patterns

Scoot and skid and jump

Twirling on a friendly edge

Vice of nice not-give-a-damn

Social open cocoon of hormones

Hoping spray paint makes someone frown

Makes someone else more human

Skate away from rulebooks

Open heart reinvention on the pavement

Skin a knee and smoke a joint, *woohoo*

Joined in kindness like nothing else matters

Except maybe fun

OLIVE TREE LEGACY

No one owns the tree, not you nor I
Reverent gratitude on borrowed time
There between the parents, earth and sky
Trees and families always seem to rhyme

> She's not just for us
>
> United and just
>
> Delighting to live
>
> Producing to give

Sit beneath her branches, taking care
Stewards earn the goodness she may bear
Rhythm shifting, different gifting grows
Deep rich dirt from where all blessing flows

> And never forget
>
> We come and we go
>
> Have not arrived yet
>
> Keep yearning to know

SHADOW ITCH

The ceilings are too low here
The walls too tight and warm
People care for too many things
Here so safe from the storm

Peek at a ka-bar from Iraq
Take out the Yarborough Knife
Old plaques and photos all dusty
Blow dust off a brutal life

A shadow yawns to stretch
At least every once in a while
What do they know of eleven bravo
Home folks in their comfortable smiles

Eighteen silence, a dozen men
Or solo on the outside now
Stretching far, you'll never hear
Letting some evil steam blow out

SWITCHING IT OFF

thinking too much
quiet now, hush

> frowner downer anyway
>
> vonnegut and hemingway
>
> crafted something good, now stop
>
> drop the bottom, blow the top
>
> empty mind and open heart
>
> thinking stop and feeling start
>
> just an hour, not all day
>
> switch it off and float away

flop on your ass
bugs in the grass
she didn't make
any mistake
made you this way
game you can play

> kid again when time left off
>
> laughing at rachmaninoff
>
> tickling beat and itching rhyme
>
> prickly heat and smell the thyme

herbs and roses, birds and bees

naked poses, dancing trees

belly dancers in your mind

sun and moon and flying blind

open the eye

facing the sky

damn it was fine

making it mine

switch it back on

find a new song

SOME THINGS

Some things, you know

Can't say them out loud

It'll whisk them into nonexistence

Morphed into what they're not

Some things

Putting them on paper is risky

Like opening a firefly jar

Like evaporating moisture from the soil

Better left as they are

Felt and undisturbed

MYSTERIOUS SONG

When each opposing side

Rises to irrational fever pitch

And each voice of kind reason

Is cast into irrelevance

The only sound to save the day

May be a primal siren song

To loosen a grip on senseless weapons

Oh, let me learn the notes of that song

Oh, let me stand and sing it long

Even if utterly alone

Even if I'm the last one

Join me or don't, but hear the notes

Oh, let me learn the song

RASH RUSH

I'm rash, I rush

Not patient much

We act, we sprint

To publish, print

What's the great hurry

Only it's fun going fast

Details of worry

Scatter right after we pass

Sprinting to each mountaintop

To stop the clock and enter heaven

Lazing there, the time is stopped

Then writing down a wafer given

I'll slow as I age

I'll chew on each bite

I'll savor the page

I'll temper the fight

But he who has the most fun wins

I aim to place

Orgasmic spasmic swimming fins

A river race

A rhyming smile of nonsense grins

Her flowing face

The earth like a body of water

A body like watery earth

All runny and funny and glistening

A rash and impatient new birth

EXPLORERS

If you've got a daredevil bug in your stomach

You'll catch my drift.

Look and see how everything decays,

Even decay itself fading

Into a process of exploration.

That's what new growth is:

Exploration.

What's over there?

Don't know? Not allowed to go?

"Frontier, here we come!"

Why? Because we can.

Drifting hidden hills and valleys,

Her forbidden body's curves

Where a wordless poem

Goes unfolding from God's mind.

We dared to explore her

Before the poem faded.

QUIET QUITTING

Enough is enough

Aren't you enough, and I

Did poetic justice to a human hammer strike

How deep the nail went we'll never know

Good thing we barely care

Got too much held up like Atlas

Good it's all now lying on the ground around us

And we sit here picking leaves apart

Neglecting to raise again the hammer

When we feel we've had enough

CITY-ZENS

A girl drops hot hotel balcony tears
Impossible to verbalize,
Pining for over-theres to be right-heres;
Plaintive straining of tired eyes,
Although as far as they can reach,
An unmet mother hides entombed.
Asphalt and concrete sneering streets
Encase her face, her breasts, her womb.

A man steers hard-bargain ego bubbles
Inaccessible to honest arts,
Shooting for taller, higher-up troubles,
Stubbornly flinging his me-darts;
Forgot what father might've said:
"Listen to your mother, boy;"
So climbs hotels until he's dead,
Scraping the sky to find some joy.

INEVITABLE AFTERNOON

It could only ever be so, say the runes

No other way could be

Exactly the weather of this afternoon

A skeptical glance aside

Shirtless working on unrhyming jokes

Matted grasses, tiny avalanches

Buried glass bottle curiosities

No longer than one or two religions ago

Inevitability wafting through

Shifting into fresher tunes

Here so many brown losses droop and fade

Fanning a background of spectacle waves

Open fields of this-is-how-it-goes

Taking a bracing half-hour or so

Shuck off memories, hang up anticipations

File funny divorce from a becoming

Lost souls stuck on table-chat mode

Light words float like seeds here

In weightless certainty of being

UN-SPOKEN WORD

Fast fad of a louder culture,
      "Spoken word" is the word of the day;
Impatient to hear a punchline,
      Force a book boy to stand up and say
That words where a silence whispers
      May as well hold their peace today,
Though maybe you read some later.
      And I pray on a spectrum they lie
Somewhere that is not top-heavy,
      Constipated, or rustic and dry,
But strum on a chord unspoken.
      In a spirit's ear let them play
            For the mind's eye.

TO THAT ONE INFANT

Hush now.
In the beginning was the baby,
You.

Beforehand,
Life is dark and vague
And quiet.

In your light, there I am
Holding you —
Dad feels like a Joseph and
Mary is mildly blank —
Diapers and laughs and
Hatching, sprout up,
Trailing me between trees,
Pumping little legs to catch up...

Till lives drift apart,
Weight piling on your back.
Never one to quit for your own good,

Barely had you caught up,
Shadowed me onto a bridge's wood,
Too high...

    long....

        Broken.

And you break to become the beginning
Of all I make that shines:

    Honest trails in trees and vines,

    Full expressions, heartfelt lines,
Long and short, low and high,

    Heavy and light; I feel your eye.
"I know," you say from the grave

    (No longer a baby's eyes).
Can you truly know what you gave?

Alone I take trails to your tree.

    Your birds' chatter is enough.

    Let no chattering camera eye intrude,

    Talkers' claims of knowing you.

    Hush.

Tomorrow, your light and noise.

But today

We quit.

Let me trail back around to holding

The beginning.

WINDINESS

A wind is one whipping in the wilderness,

"Weave straight the way through willow switches"

Brittle branches o' whippoorwill tunes

Whistling away, wishing, washing yesterday

Sandblast stripped us of winning whispers

"Waste-not-want-not" broke and blew away

    Scattered letters got captured

    In thorny continuity

    Dried-up leaves awaited the rapture

    But founded fans of vanity

Wilderness zones, deaf tunes, disposable homes

A long view forward takes a long look back

Sounds and senses, resurrected but dim

Even in defeat the eloquent don't lack

Earth and heaven yet connected by Him

As less-lettered tribes are supplanted

(To chase fairness is striving after wind)

Windiness latterly was locally diffused

In language, stories, songs of the muse

Airy unknowns are breezily true

But not as heavy as dust devils

Whereby my way shall be to eschew

Well-known bell-rings of the high levels

Nor spew a balancing lie to you

Though many live high on that sort of diet

Come to the city wall and be quiet

  To be civilized while not a snob

  Well-booked while not a bore

  A workhorse but rarely a slob

(Nor slave of I-wish-I-could-buy-it)

  To have less and yet be more

Possessions blow away

And so do we

Nostalgia's throw-away

Until we're free

  Like the air and rain and dust

  Fiery sun and fiery lust

  Watery eye and windy gust

There in the eye of a Nineveh sandstorm

Where faces could barely stand
Was found in one gravelly crouching
As fingers confront the sand
It hands you a gritty licking
Whirling and hurling it whips
Ripping, spattering, sticking
Chapping and cracking your lips

How much rain went wasted
Unloved, unsaved, untasted
How many homes disposed, letters penned
For a windy desert to win in the end?

AND ANOTHER THAT'S HARD TO NAME

And they say not to start
Any sentence with "And"
As if practiced beginnings
Are why sentences stand.

I'm a rube with a dearth
Of the commas and dots;
Only pauses and endings
Frame the worthiest thoughts....

    (And now and again
    Old walls ought to stand.)
    Here's two eyes, two ears
    Only one writing hand
Five large senses and all this skin
Just three fingers to hold a pen
Big brain, big world of instinct, do, think
But one sore wrist and a tiny tube of ink

From misplaced beginnings and periods,

Where stopping aborts the mysterious,
Oh Lord, in your grace, deliver us.

Of cultures that run on conceits
(Proper flops defeat sloppy new feats)
Oh, help us depose the priests.

From numinal fixated homages
For temples erected of loneliness,
Oh midwife of gods, deliver us.

From obsessive amalgamation
As from reckless disintegration,
Pray save a pubescent nation.

To pride that's taken in spots
Where duties are higher than thoughts,
Oh heaven, abandon us not.

     Place a period upon the pen of the man
          Who finds no redemption inherent
          In movements of heirs apparent;

And grace with a couple of pauses

      The hasty sensations impatient

      To delete old civilizations.

At a point,

A free verse fails to stand

If deprived of skeletal structure,

So it joins

A framing built on land

Made fertile by its rupture.

We've yet to fill earth's cavities,

Have yet to answer gravity

      With concrete of Roman integrity,

Though we suffer no dearth of sand

For the mixing of mortar by hand,

      While writing a flagstone word—"And".

PAUSE

Best at the end of the day
And blessed when you rest and let go
Pause throwing feelings away
At folks who would rather not know
Many won't speak the same tongue
And pearls may be pebbles at times
Don't blame the hasty and young
Who scatter the lights of their minds
Not even age is in touch
With senses forgotten since birth
Sometimes the years add too much
Mistaking the baggage with worth
Crawl with a child and just smile
At jokes that will never grow old
Walk in the dark for a while
What's yours you can silently hold

New Year's Eve

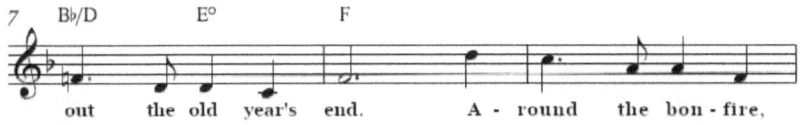

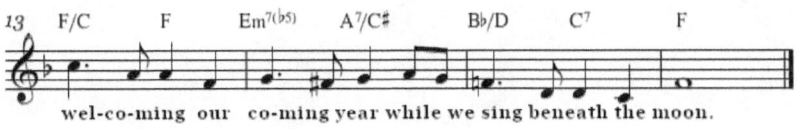

Adapted from a translation of the ancient Welsh carol "Nos Galan",
matched to the familiar Scottish tune of Auld Lang Syne.

PART 3

STRIPPING NAMELESS

O

The youthfully agile
     Come pick the ripened things,
All working and joking,
     All reaches, bends, and leans.

In harvest we're sorting
     When picking is complete.
The bad ones are compost,
     The ugly are to eat,
The good ones for sharing,
     The pretty for the store.
But the highest in beauty
     We plant and grow some more.

A store shelf or table
Won't honor them enough.
     Like youth and desire,
     Not wasting them is tough.

The only solution
Is sticking them in dirt
　　Like a ripened desire,
　　Not like a harmless flirt.

1

Your inner adrenaline junkie

Every FTW fling

Hang gliding over fjords

Take the aching loss and send it flying

It could smolder and hollow you out

Or shoot out to the infinite

Thrills all through the veins

Spine chills, goosebumps

Before you bury it all proper

    Take it on the wild rides

        Become who you always were inside

            Freefalling into the core

                Of everything that is

2

In prison you're given a number

Your name no longer matters

And your art is erased every hour

At least that's what I guess from out here

I can't know the rough canvas

Nor can you

Till you've been

In the darkest recesses of the soul

In animal survival mode

A nameless twilight zone

Links dragging in dungeons of

Iron and concrete and numbers

Numb, numb, numbers

3

Of making many books there is no end,

Yet even illiterate eyes

May one day meander across

Poetry scrawled over a few dozen acres

Off Riverton Road,

Authored by Mother Earth

With us little co-contributors.

Nothing written on pages will ever compare.

If I'm ever in heaven,

You'll find me there.

4

You can communicate volumes

Without ever expressing yourself

It's easy and unfortunate

Folks do it all the time

All it takes is not knowing yourself

I just did that yesterday

Skipped out on the best knowing there is

Forgot the best release there is

Unfortunate

5

Lower notes vibrate to shake foundations
Like loneliness being fire we play in
Along the way to forge a key to happiness
Communication is not the key

      Until you've opened the mind to see
      Do-good pretense is a mockery
      To blow hot air will not set us free

You may be warm in company
King of the hour or queen of the party
Tight team around a table

      But out there at lower decibels
      In the background lies the foolish profound
      Its larger amplitudes lie buried in loud crowds

The key is in me where also lies
The linking to you and to those outside
Dragging a chain where I thought I was free
Relishing now the connection

      Solitude brought a collection to me
      Collecting the thoughts of creation

Happiness taps on a higher-pitched key

Where circumstances delight us

But lower notes are the air now to breathe

Let me exhale onto your leaves

A gibberish you may digest and filter

Seeping down to the roots

6

Gut-wrenching story
Old guts and glory
Gory fairy tales all true
Got nothing to do with you
Or everything

When do they end
The gutsy trends
To pitch us into each other
The fratricide, brother to brother

So, you kneel to Allah and I don't
And I'm wrong and so are you
Struggling gut-check time
Get over it

Wrench out of the stories
Into a tale of you and me
Standing to spot land

Dropping anchor to shake hands

Choosing to be free

Some would kill us for this

And one day they might

But we're alright

Guts got everything to do with it

7

Check the time, tick, tick

Inhale, and...

"Shots fired, shots fired!"

Nope, no holes here

Somehow it wasn't my turn

"Hands, hands, show your hands!"

Thank the fates, I guess

The deed itself

Never dripped from my fingers

Not for lack of trying

To find the wrong place and time

Check your six again, Anakim

Giant storm cloud forms ahead

Nature culls the herd again

Head on a swivel, iron and lead

Bloodshot mind's abyss

On other shots, thinking only makes you tired

I still found the insomnia somehow
Heavy metal fog in the head
In gunsmoke the tidy plans expire
Haywire comes on clouds of glory
Don't shoot the messenger
Please don't praise him either

You can only roll the dice but so many times before
Shouldering burdens you shirked
Working hair-trigger nerves
Bedtime is when it all hits
And whiskey tango fox, surrender the results
What was it all for anyway

It's 2 a.m. here
Here's hoping the fates hold steady
But still, my hands are not unstained
Breathe in and out and roll with it and
Have a silent drink with me

8

Who ever said,

    "I love you, so

    I'm going to utterly control you,

    Take away everything you knew and had,

    Scrape and cut the familiar life out of you,

    Force you to give only my immediate wants"?

And how can I say,

    "I love this land"

While approving endeavors

To do all those things to the land?

9

The forest is fluent

In a language you and I forgot

It hates getting burned

But sometimes loves it oh so much

Saying "it" doesn't feel right

Not sure where pronouns enter the woods

Moses' burning sky god

Is just as male as the earth is female

And that's real

I may be all grizzly and gruff

But even the most feminine you

Is part of me

And the gruffest masculine me

Is part of you

Womanly as you may be

And the forest is our kin

I think the word for "kin"

Sounds like a birdsong I heard today

10

You there, blue jay fleeing

Flittering between scrub oaks

All bright and noisy

Tattling to the others

"A human is here! A human is here!"

Your feathers in the mottled light

Darting out from yellow and purple wildflowers

How did you all get so beautiful?

I love you

You there exclusive and private

Human reading this alone

Your eyes

They're blinding me

How did so much life get in them?

When will you let it out?

Light goes in, life flows out

Something going on in there

I don't know how you do it without trying

You're a portal without thinking

You there, somehow

I guess I love you, too

11

It's howling out there
But the windchimes provide no
Magic tonight, no release
Dog snores in dreamless sleep
Cat is bored of trifles
And here I write my drivel
Time chuckles, and still no release
What is it needs releasing?
You're holding a howling wolf by the ears
It was rarely about hate, really
People don't naturally hate forever
No, it's in the profits
People want more forever
And how do you release a "more" animal?
By denying its nature?
Nobody really hates the nature
Profit motives only tangled with her
Complex nets choke a child's simple release
But mother nature is no wolf

Even if she bites—yes

And there it is

You know I like it when she bites

12

A child might dream

      Of secret gardens and green foreign fields

      And may the sweet dreams not die

A mother might dream

      Of exotic new seed planted in her own garden

      And why on earth not?

A man might dream

      Of sowing wild oats around the world

      May he never repent of the dreams

13

What's in a name
What's in a word
Blurt it out all around

 Time, turn, spin

 Spinnnn! Spin-in-in-in...

 Stuck, rut

 Ruth, ruthless, root

 Roots are where it's at

Interpret, think, feel, remember
All so familiar and circular
This word over that, love over power
All just blurted words?
Names for spinning thoughts?

 A thought's a thing

 And so is a root

 And so is a word

Things so plain and little
Some of them sometimes somehow
Become timeless

14

The dirt is black and richer here
More red and sticky there
Like reddish necks of Scots who came
And plowed it up, and gave it care

From too much care it's lying bare
Like used-up prostitutes
A strip mall here, a highway there
Accustomed to our heavy boots

From bare white sand to black or red
Forgiveness bleeds from earth
Brown dirt is in our fingernails
The deep red dirt is giving birth

15

They bounce around judgements on
"The highest and best use for that land"
      Judgements based on what
      Dollars or factors of city planning?
      "Wisdom" one century old?
What of wisdom embedded in a land
Living and breathing for countless millennia
Since before any European knew it was there
Before any Lumbee or Tuscarora passed through
      Highest and best what?
      How about tuning in to hear the land on
      Her highest and best use for humans
Arrogant newcomers, all of us
Judges in kangaroo courts

ding...

The church bells only chime by day
And serious times are not for play

dong...

For daytime people of the book
The legends written, come and look

ding...

It's neat and clean and orthodox
And fits inside a tidy box

dong...

All-Father God, all rigid claims
No Mother Earth, no birthing pains

ding...

The church bell sermon looming large
So loud and steady and in charge

dong...

"Deny the night and rule the day
Burn all the heretics away"

ding...

17

Feed me more
I feed, I draw, I extract your energy
To churn it up within me
Return it ten times as heady to you
A hundredfold as life-sustaining
As when it flowed to me
Through look or bodily touch
I wish I could love a person
As easily as I love a dog's smile
Or respect you as simply
As I respect a cat's instinct
But too much noise gets between us
Just have to look or touch through it all
And feed each other

18

Don't know why I like it but I do

Somebody's gotta sweat it

Yanking down some parasitic vines

      Disentangle a mesh to squeeze

      Tight spaces between sharp trees

Giving work to a forest I owe

Gift cycles in perpetual motion

Only do it if it's fun

Fun is goodness in purest state

      What else does a mind exist for

      If not to receive all the goodness and more

Liking to express it back in turn

      But parasitic habits never grasped

      Reciprocating bonding tasks

Though I never aim to end the vines

Beings in their own right, or basket material

They gave me, the newcomer, some grapes today

But their limit comes around as the gifts

Everyone's limit comes around

Frolicking between excess and restraint.

19

Death was whirling through the mind
Silently smothering toward oblivion
I grabbed a shovel and started digging
Clods of earth flew by my ears
Outwardly self-contained
Inside impatient raving

"Get me down there now, shovels!
Let me, let me go down with him
Down with the brother I should've been"

My mind churning, barely hearing the earth
Whispering, saving, speaking life
What she spoke can never translate to English
But part of it goes something like this

"You don't need so many shovels
He's here and he's my son, too
I won't give him back, but

I'm giving you a whole new world"

She used what I had already
What made no sense to me
Used it to do her mending
Knowing exactly where to stitch

20

Moon light
Will you come and kiss me goodnight
Moon light
Saying everything is alright

When I'm feeling my way
When I'm flailing today
Will you hear when I pray

Moon light
Will you come and kiss me goodnight
Moon light
Saying everything is alright

21

Stand at the first fall firepit

Turn north and wade in gently

Slide between some elder ones

Follow the deer steps down

Passing under the widowmaker

Where a juniper brightly greets you

Cross a tiny valley of death

Holly helps you up the other side

To cease and center yourself

How did the fire ants know

We came to attack their pines

I'm just a bigger ant, god complex on the outside

Root mounds recline to mark it

In here is the pressure point

Where all the outside circumscribing

Feels its heart

And at last, she appeared by surprise

The moon smiling down

Through the widowmaker's branches

22

Scratch when it itches

Unhesitating

Stop when it doesn't

Or you'll be bleeding

The knowing yourself is a threshold

But losing yourself is the entrance

Down into the caverns of mystery

And words we know not how to mention

> "Mystery," they're scoffing

> "Everything's an open door"

> Age of information

> Shifting shadows are no more

> Never comes another

> Dim Taliesin, murky lore

I'll not be wasting a letter

Proving, persuading

But for a few of the scratchers

Diamonds are waiting

23

I was a cell in an ocean's mind

Demanding new land

Amending, emitting new mends

Commending, commanding a space unmanned

New-word thoughts in meanings

Non-word knots turning solid

Awen weaving liquid word-tangles

New World feelings in flight

To and from, Mind and Land

Where new MAND will stand

And the sunny male fire-keepers looked

And the earthy female water-keepers laughed

Androgynous wind blew restlessly

Elusive, forever inconclusive

Across the face of something that was nothing

But at least more solid now

Than the older ocean waves

24

Given up, a rearview mirror

Gorchfygu, defeated, conquered

Grampa's nation/tongue

Burned and flowed and sung

Eight hundred weary years of prayers

"Savior, expel the greedy invaders"

Stories in chest-thumping, unbreaking themes

Free-swinging tongues that were bloody sharp things

And now my tongue is colonized

And here two separate words divide

A "nation" from a "language"

Old flames are long extinguished

Old syllables gave themselves freely

To poetry, much like a lady

Giving herself to a warrior youth

Dropping an ego, embracing a truth

That unity isn't so bad

Though something will always be lost

For natural gains to be had

But somehow a rhythm is tossed

Far up from a myth in the mist

To colonized tongues that unite

When tonight in a union we rest

When we got here by losing a fight

I'm no Homer, no courtyard bard

Home is humbler, more honest by far

While poor lost winners always wander

All blind and tone deaf, drifting yonder

Eyes off the rearview

Our road is asphalt

Blackwater hinterlands

Come to a halt

Bald cypress and muscadines dangle

All tangled in stubborn old glory

Where Henry B. Lowry paddled

A worn-out new stream of a story

25

Brawling thunder boys
Spirits of pounding sound
Force of fist and noise
Racing voices shaking ground

Destruction runs faster than creation
Is that what you want?
More destruction?
Slow down, sit down
Find the balance slamming down in music
Of brawling thunder boys

One hand gives in grace
Other one makes a fist
Pounds the louder pace
Faster beat, run drumming on this

26

"Whispering, whispering
We are the moon people
The night's own
Drifting in dripping dew
Gentle folk, but
In a flicker, then invisible
Fear us not, except
Only listen
Very nearly all inaudible
Where our branching shadows go
Whispering, whispering"

27

Grateful to this soil

    Bringing oceans of life to sibling trees

    Life to family and neighbors

Grateful to these roots

    Breathing living wisdom all around

    Beside me and through me

Grateful to those branches

    Sharing strength and shade

    Food and beauty

Grateful to the breezy air

    Carrying golden pollen

    Sex between food-givers

Grateful to this water

    Sustaining flow of Earth's body

    Milk from the holy nipple

Grateful to the sun

     Spreading Creator spirit generously

     Drying up varied old evils

Grateful to forest trails

     Washing the soul clean

     Bathing me in a walk

Grateful to this moment

This drop in the ocean of time

28

She was the beating heart of her family for decades,

Or would've been if she'd ever put down her phone.

He was a pillar of the community,

Or would've been if he'd ever showed up for things.

They were credible, well-versed, solid,

If only they'd ever bothered to read whole books.

Radiant, vibrant humans,

If only they'd allowed for sexual inspiration.

What the hell is wrong with us all anyway?

29

If making is better than breaking
Then why is breaking so fun?
So natural-feeling and easy?
So thrilling a race to run?

The only piece that makes
    This puzzle resolve,
    This question dissolve,
Is how good making takes
    A big thrilling course
    Of sexual force.

30

Easy Dionysian side of life
And then sweating the other side
Up and at 'em, zig and zag
Climbing a mountain with no summit
At least I hope we never arrive to stop
The final top would end the party

31

From the shadow wrinkle regions
Crannies and nooks of my mind
To your corresponding dungeons
Stretches a spiderweb twine

Pulses humming down that thread
Hither and thither between
Let us know we're not quite dead
Yet things are not as they seem

Folds and creases find each other
Down the inscrutable line
Showing how you're known by another
And that my mind is not mine

32

What Cain did to Abel

Israelites did to Canaanites

Romans did to everyone

Monotheists to heathens

English to native Britons

Then later to native Americans

Moors and Portuguese did to sub-Saharans

Colonists to indigenous everywhere

Natives to immigrants everywhere

Turks to Armenians, Nazis to Jews, Hutus to Tutsis,

Serbs to Bosniaks, Islamists to Yezidis

What brother does to brother ceaselessly

Since the earliest tribes eyed each other

Is what we do to ourselves

When each dawn greets a man's bottomless greed

And how long can a race continue

To treat itself this way?

33

Look at the roots making love, digging in

To soft-skinned sandhills down home

In the Old North State,

While branches spread around the world.

Wide wanderings have their place

Whose full range must not be denied,

But I never heard of babies born with shoes on.

Unless ye become as a little child

Ye shall not enter the kingdom of heaven.

Grownup child, look where you're lying;

This here is holy ground,

So take off your clothes

And let's put down roots.

34

Did you know
While they wondered why
We didn't join the fray
I was busy drawing a circle
Around the whole pissing contest
Buying up the whole joint
With silent, invisible currency
So snap to, straighten up now
I'm the unofficial landlord
Move on, idiot warmongers
There's other places to piss

35

She's not spectacular to the well-traveled

This sandhills land, not at first

No ancient stone wonders

No mountaintops of mosquito-free breeze

She's humble and heavily used in spots

But all it takes is a grove or riverbank

Where hardwoods hold an upper hand

To see where she's found herself again

Returned to the glory of lush, thick growth

Nearly impenetrable canvasses of cascading life

36

That man knows how to

Serve his god

He drains a swamp to

Grow his sod

He finds a living

Breathing place

Then kills it, makes it

Real estate

Rips out green creatures

Ages old

Plants others he can

Best control

What fed a magic

Consciousness

Now trades in dollars

And hubris

Without a thought of

"Thanks" or "please"

His Mammon god must

Be appeased

The lord of money

Takes a soul

Makes in its place a

Gaping hole

37

Lying in a timeless clearing

Sending messages through time

Hey you, fancy future people

   If you have to come and build here

   Build a shrine to what was here

  Before you built your silly shrine

Lying heavy on my eyelids

He who has the eyes to read

Let him heed the gift, accepting

   Though you kick a wooden manger

   Keep the baby, care for her

  And let her shine, and meet her needs

38

You're racking your brain all for what
Come lifting a load from the mind
Don't come here with something to prove
Come only to leave it behind
The mental and spiritual dust
May cling to the shoes of the frail
Before you transcend, it must be
Replaced by the dust of the trail

39

You fellow life-breathers, my scattered tribe,

Challenge me, put me to shame,

And I in turn will challenge you.

You who mean to embrace the world,

Have you found how to reach the ends?

The easternmost east, the westernmost west;

And what of the center?

More to the point, what of longitude?

Have you folded both far poles into your soul?

You man who would pierce the mystic depths,

Have you imbibed the female principle into yourself?

You woman who would encompass the core of
existence,

Have you absorbed the male principle in its entirety?

Before you paint me yin and yang,

Do you feel them fully in the spirit and the flesh?

40

Marooned on a moonlit slope
Mountains of sundown
Red shades of a fading hope
Dye the moon's nightgown

In moonlight the buck is out
Antlers impressive
He stares at me, standing proud
Bellows his message

I follow him with the eye
Buckhorns in cold air
I cannot translate the night
Had to have been there

41

You say you believe

A story stern

The righteous will leave

The world will burn

And yet at your sleeve

A golden urn

The Rolex is fine

That's not the thing

Just thinking of time

And reckoning

A kingdom divine

And smaller things

You claim that you aim

Through needle's eyes

And yet you attain

A camel's size

Enough will remain

Be satisfied

42

Pride got a bad rap indeed
By sharing a bed with greed
    And the marriage has been sealed
    In American ideals
Praise the Union from which
Blessings flow, but there's a hitch
    Where a greedy squirrel stowed
    Far more nuts than he was owed
Fool with a jittery soul
Tonight giving back what he stole
    When his God required an account
    And a bobcat spit the tail out
Never neuter a wildcat's pride
But know the difference deep inside
    His God may be the same one
    That kicks a couple from Eden
    For taking though they had it all
    It's greed that doth precede the fall
Now comes a time of divorce
May pride go charting a wiser course

43

Bright fruits

Dark greens

White fish

Black beans

Contrast

Fills you

And feeds

Me too

44

Ba-ba-bom, ba-ba-bom

Ba-ba-bom, bagaba-ba-bom

Drum the one, sun is down

Count the number, the sum of sound

Come all round, hear the drum

Feel a pounding, a grounding hum

Da-da-dom, da-da-dom

Da-da-dom, dagada-da-dom

Beating long, bringing home

Throbbing song that a body's known

Find a zone, follow strong

Hollow bone on a ringing gong

Ga-ga-gone, ga-ga-gone

Ga-ga-gone, gabaga-ga-gone

45

Their cosmology is true

Though it somehow caught a flu

And then somehow so is mine

Though it's running out of time

Sprinting feverishly hard

Begging karma, "Show your cards"

How can this and that be so

How could anybody know

Their mythology is right

Other symbols shine a light

While a darkness they despise

Holds a kernel deep and wise

And the tempo of a beat

Marks a truth of stamping feet

While a melody on high

Brings a burning from the sky

Seeing that and holding this

Being bad to follow bliss

Till it opens unseen doors

Thinking less and feeling more

46

Have you found your forbidden ecstasy?

Have you dreamed of it, quiet, next to me?

Notch the arrow

Let it fly

Knock the fear down

From the sky

47

Thank you for making rules

Perfect for snapping in half

Glory, glory, hallelujah

Words are a crayon fragment

And I will not stay inside the lines

Departure is a shade darker

Than folks are comfy with

Excellent, says I

Keeping comfy is overrated

And rules are for breaking

If you're my people

You'll say amen

48

Spilt white milk and worshipping a book
Seed spilled on the road in a parable
Walking rocky steps under a load
Knees ache when they never bend
The easy yoke and light burden
Didn't need to include so much paper
Something about black and white options
A certain few steeple people won't get a grip
Keep saying "read here" and "look there"
When it's spread out in us already
But they're stuck between the covers
Of the milk of the book words

49

When in the course

Of human events

Papers get written

Thoughts given vent

Air out a spirit

Of breaking away

Breathe in its nostrils

The breath of the day

Inhale the red brick-dust

Exhale a design

Draw plans in the sawdust

Erect us a shrine

      But how much can the dust of the ground

      Hold up the whole structure, how sound

      How firm a foundation that stands

      On compulsory labor in stolen lands

      When your Protestant work ethic won't

      Work anymore, then just don't

Human events

Inhuman empires

Erecting ideals

Till humans expire

Natural building

Unnaturally tall

Resources seizing

Expending it all

       Events better tend to redeem in the end

       Give nature her resources, heal and defend

50

When the sound is just right,
You feel it somewhere
Around the salivary glands
As something olfactory tags a memory
You can never place in time,
And somewhere down along a vibrating cord,
Another you has an orgasm,
When the sound is just right.

51

Notebook pages come loose of the binding

Lost leaves will never be matched

Epic stories where half is forgotten

Where eggs of dragons were hatched

Football field of a pigskin pass

Or maybe a rugby pitch

Footwork meadows of knee-high grass

And hopping a mound or ditch

Binding twisting of willow branches

We're bound in location and sound

Twisting tongues or a wordless drumbeat

We're tied by the life in the ground

Then here back into the pen-training prose or else tongue practicing noises that nobody knows more delicate melodies spurt and then flow when you're not holding back what you have to let go—you have to let go—you have to let go so much to be found in learning to send the same messages in so many different ways even if nobody believes what you create no frowners can take away what's already received by light of day for better or worse the delicacies stick in consciousness biding their time kids won't get it but then again they will and by the time they do you've already had your fill tear down this boundary wall us and them old and young capital and lower case-ism all separate lines to rhyme but no more for a time to practice scattering former backbeats and just for a moment replacing them with nothing and god bless this in your moment of holy-cow melody.

53

When time has piled them up to date

Memories on memories, early and late

The layers fall, year in, year out

Leaves in a woodland, shuffling about

They settle, morphing, then unite

Living, reliving, cozy and tight

In warm defiance undefined

In bare reliance, all combined

Then time will come around to see

Life over death, like you over me

54

Big adult life is more

Of a horrible bore

Than the high ones would like to admit

If you start to not care

Then come down from up there

And you may find salvation from it

55

I think I found the spot
Where the land likes to be tickled.
Let's hang out there a lot;
We can stand, lie down or wiggle.

Let's make a hobbit hole;
We'll be rough, barefoot and cozy,
Eat acorns that we stole,
Watch the sky blushing all rosy.

I find I just can't stop.
Feel the place; seems like a portal.
And when the sun has dropped,
Then she breathes, lying immortal.

56

Can't get enough of that you
Can't get enough of that they
Can't get enough of...
And on and on along it runs
An endless cycle 'round the sun
The wings will melt, I'm not a dove
If greed must be, be greedy for love

57

Distilled lessons?
Condensed thought?
Spare us, heavens
Allow it not
But rather gifting
Shapeshifting, no rules
Transcendence twisting
To shapes, using tools
Of language on paper
A thought-tainted thing
Then moments later
Break through, taking wing

Need edginess be the payment that bought
       Uneven proofs of mettle?
Might restless depth of feeling or thought
       Keep deep and yet be settled?

          Unsettling is the choice
          "Be weak or else be wicked"
          Expected to raise a voice
          Sing hymns to a relic or kick it

On opposite banks are settled old chaps
       Of smokestack ivory towers
Who chuckle at us provincial hacks
       And decline to smile at flowers

          Dilemmas are not for them
          Their neighbors are more meaty
          No choices are needed when
          They've drafted an eloquent treaty

They've read every mind from Virgil to Kant
      While looking down their noses
At us peasants who claim to know what we want
      Or believe in Christ or Moses

          While here on an in-between edge
          Small tyranny amuses
          While planting my wicked-ish hedge
          I'm not the man who chooses

59

Who writes his brother a poem? Who?
It's simply not what the normal do.
     Please call me weird
     And laugh out loud;
     At last we've veered
     Out from the crowd.
A zombie mob with its blinders on
Has never got what a father's son
     Or brother's brother
     Has got to know;
     They'd rather smother
     Than let him go.
"Release the letters," I said to me,
And me protested, but let it be.
     We're each constricted
     Within our rhyme,
     Each rhythm rigid
     Just keeping time.
In space our race is a desperate strain;

We run in sun, and we run in rain.

      Quick brother, you

      Are running well.

      I hope you knew

      A truth I tell:

On acreage there where you build a home,

Which hums at night as you walk alone,

      Where family's buzz

      May make you warm

      And dry because

      You'll beat the storm,

I wish I could walk a mile with you

Each day when all of the buzz is through,

      While we're still breathing

      And fit to hike

      And hum, relieving

      What life is like.

60

The raves are my shovels
But some of them break
In youth I dig faster
For energy's sake
One day it will mellow
We'll broaden the cave
Unless it collapses
And nothing is saved

61

Rifling through life's pages

Hunting down a challenge

Pep talk, a proof, a talent

The ladder steps in stages

Strike the ladder down

Rip some pages out

Wheel the hunt about

Forget about renown

Take a page and walk

To find a thing to crave

And ride it to the grave

Ignoring all the talk

62

It was 20 below freezing
    Christmas week.
My experimental projects
    Cannot speak.
Avocado trees and citrus
    Freeze and grieve,
Or have gone the way of winter,
    Taking leave.

I'll experiment again when
    Springtime shines;
Darwin's law will be my partner
    In more crimes.
Thank the cold VA Department
    For some seed;
Life and taxes buy me lemons
    In my need.

In materialistic flurries

Christmas died,

But the solstice and the New Year

Stay alive;

Braving flashy plastic blizzards

Next time 'round,

I'll retire to build a fire

On the ground.

63

Like fingernails on chalkboard,
Like rubbing Styrofoam,
Is prose that someone dragged into
A neat poetic form.
I'm sorry to have mixed in
A couple of these beasts
Like cockroaches in caviar,
Like vomit at a feast.
An urge to state a concept,
An itching to converse,
Occasionally pokes into
The spirit of a verse.
Some others have been guilty
Of this in every line;
At least with me a fingernail
Can break in quicker time.

64

It thumps—my heart—it pumps—inside

 "pulsate—pulsate—pulsate—pulsate"

A stomping beat, a bumpy ride

 "don't wait, don't wait, don't wait, don't wait"

Not flying high, but riding low

 vibrate—vibrate—vibrate—vibrate

I cannot hate the rhythm's flow

 no hate, no hate, no hate, no hate

The beat, a thrust; the flow, a kiss

 relate—relate—relate—relate

Relating with creation's bliss

 create, create, create, create

www.ingramcontent.com/pod-product-compliance
Lightning Source LLC
Chambersburg PA
CBHW021613120626
46545CB00001B/201